OLYMPIC REALITIES
SECHS STÄDTE NACH DEM GROSSANLASS
BRUNO HELBLING (HRSG.)

OLYMPIC REALITIES
SIX CITIES AFTER THE GAMES
BRUNO HELBLING (ED.)

BIRKHÄUSER
BASEL

INHALT

CONTENTS

ATHEN 1896 & 2004
OLYMPISCHE SOMMERSPIELE

Eine grandiose Fete und
ein langer, langer Hangover

Essay von Werner van Gent

ATHENS 1896 & 2004
SUMMER OLYMPICS

A Splendid Celebration and
a Long, Enduring Hangover

Essay by Werner van Gent

Es war an einem sonnenüberfluteten Dienstag, nur zehn Wochen vor der offiziellen Eröffnung der Olympischen Spiele, als die Medien zum OAKA, dem Olympia-Sportkomplex Athen in Maroussi, gerufen wurden.

Das OAKA war zu diesem Zeitpunkt noch eine gigantische Baustelle. Das Velodrom war gerade erst fertiggestellt worden, vor dem Leichtathletik- und Tenniszentrum wurde noch heftig gegraben und asphaltiert und im Wassersportzentrum war die Kontroverse um das fehlende Dach über dem Außenschwimmbecken noch lange nicht ausgestanden. Nur vor dem Spiros-Louis-Stadion ruhten die Bautrupps. Und doch spürte man rasch, dass hier gerade ein Stück Geschichte geschrieben wurde. An diesem Tag würde sich nämlich entscheiden, ob die große Wette aufgehen oder das denkbar größte Desaster über Athen hereinbrechen würde. Tage zuvor schon hatte man mit den Vorbereitungen begonnen, um die zwei gigantischen Stahlbögen der Dachkonstruktion von Stararchitekt Santiago Calatrava mit überdimensionierten hydraulischen Zuggeräten von zwei Seiten her über das Stadion zu ziehen. Ein waghalsiges Unterfangen. Wenn nur eine Pumpe versagt oder, noch schlimmer, sich die gigantische Stahlkonstruktion verkantet hätte, hätten die Spiele ohne Dach eröffnet werden müssen – auf welche Blamage, welch homerisches Gelächter hätte man sich einstellen müssen!

Wenige Monate zuvor hatte Denis Oswald, Präsident des Organisationskomitees des IOC, angesichts der immer neuen Probleme und der immer längeren Verzögerungen beim Bau des Daches sichtlich entnervt gesagt, für das Gelingen der Spiele sei das Dach nicht zwingend nötig. Doch ein halbes Dach? Oder eine schiefe Konstruktion? Zu viel hing zu diesem Zeitpunkt bereits vom Gelingen der Operation ab. Damit die insgesamt 19 000 Tonnen schweren Bögen nicht einsacken würden, hatte man zwei Kabeltunnel, welche das Stadion mit dem International Broadcast Centre (IBC) verbanden, kurzerhand

1 – Das Olympiastadion «Spiros Louis» vom Leichtathletik-Trainingszentrum aus gesehen.

2 – Eine verwitterte Plakatsäule im Olympiapark.

It was a sunny Tuesday, only ten weeks before the official opening of the Olympic Games, when the media were summoned to the OAKA, the Athens Olympic Sports Complex in Maroussi.

At this point, the OAKA was still a gigantic construction site. The Velodrome had just been finished, frantic digging and asphalt work was going on in front of the Athletics and Tennis Centre, and in the Aquatic Centre, the heated debate about the missing roof above the outdoor swimming pools was far from over. Only in front of the Spiros Louis Stadium, the construction units were resting their tools. And still one could feel that a piece of history was in the making. It was the day which would decide whether the audacious gamble would pay off or the biggest disaster imaginable would descend upon Athens. Several days before, preparations had begun to draw two gigantic steel arches that belonged to the roof construction designed by star architect Santiago Calatrava on

top of the stadium from two sides, using oversize hydraulic towing equipment. Quite a bold venture. If just one pump failed or, even worse, the gigantic steel construction tilted, the organisers would be forced to open the Games without a roof – just imagine the humiliation, the Homeric laughter that would ensue!

Only a few months before that moment, a visibly exasperated Denis Oswald, president of the IOC Organising Committee, had said that in light of the never-ending problems and repeatedly extended delays in the construction of the roof, said roof might not be an essential requirement for the success of the Games. But half a roof? Or a lopsided construction? At that moment in time, too much already depended on the success of the operation. To ensure that the 19,000 tons of heavy arches would not subside, two cable tunnels, which connected the stadium to the International Broadcast Centre (IBC), had been covered in concrete without further ado.

These tunnels would only be bared again after the successful positioning of the roof, which caused some grumbling within the IBC. Many kilometres of cable had yet to be installed in order to let the world public witness the opening ceremony.

Safety issues were raised until the very end, as for lack of time, the construction project had been contracted out before the wind tunnel studies had been completed. When these studies were finally submitted, it turned out that the construction had some weak spots. On very short notice the diameter of the steel arches had to be widened from 2.4 to 3.6 metres, which in turn necessitated the redimensioning of the foundations. This in turn unveiled that the floor analyses had not been sufficiently rigorous. New probes uncovered frighteningly brittle layers. Technical inspectors produced calculations that revealed a realistic danger that the two 70-metre-long tracks, which would serve to push the

Essay von Werner van Gent

zubetonieren lassen. Diese Tunnel würden erst nach vollendeter Positionierung des Daches freigelegt werden, was im IBC wiederum zu roten Köpfen führte. Kilometerlange Kabel mussten noch verlegt werden, damit die Weltöffentlichkeit der Eröffnungszeremonie beiwohnen könnte.

Bis zuletzt hatte es zudem Sicherheitsbedenken gegeben, weil der Bauauftrag aus Zeitgründen noch vor dem Abschluss von Windkanalstudien vergeben worden war. Als diese endlich vorlagen, stellten sich Schwachstellen in der Konstruktion heraus. Kurzfristig musste der Diameter der Stahlbögen von 2,4 auf 3,6 Meter vergrößert werden, was wiederum eine Redimensionierung der Fundamente nötig machte. Dabei zeigten sich die Bodenanalysen als nicht umfassend genug. Neue Proben hatten erschreckend morsche Schichten aufgedeckt. Kontrollingenieure rechneten vor, es bestünde eine reale Gefahr, dass die beiden 70 Meter langen Geleise, über welche die Bögen mitsamt der ausgefeilten Dachkonstruktion aus Glas über das Stadion geschoben werden sollten, einsacken oder gar einknicken könnten – mit desaströsen Folgen für die Dachkonstruktion. Manch einer dürfte sich in jenen Tagen gewünscht haben, es beim alten, langweiligen und in die Jahre gekommenen Stadion belassen zu haben. Doch die Bögen mussten nicht nur das Glasdach, sondern auch die gesamte Licht- und Audiotechnik tragen. So kurz vor dem Beginn der Spiele gab es kein Zurück mehr.

Der spanische Stararchitekt Santiago Calatrava zeigte sich unbeeindruckt von der wachsenden Kritik. Sein Dach werde rechtzeitig fertig sein, ließ er gegenüber den Medien verlauten.

Die an diesem Tag versammelten Medien waren diesbezüglich geteilter Meinung. Diejenigen, die sich eine problemlose Sportfeier wünschten, schauten mit leichtem Entsetzen auf die zweimal 70 Meter, welche noch zurückzulegen waren. Die übrigen malten sich saftige

3 — Der Westeingang zum Olympiapark in Athen, der öffentlich zugänglich ist.

arches, along with the sophisticated glass roof construction, on top of the stadium, might subside or even fold – with disastrous consequences for the roof construction. In these days of turmoil, many probably wished they would have made do with the old, boring and ageing stadium. The arches, however, did not only have to carry the glass roof, but also the entire light and audio technology. Such a short time before the opening of the Games, there was no way back.

The Spanish star architect Santiago Calatrava was little impressed with the growing criticism, telling the media that his roof would be finished in time.

The views of the media representatives present that day were divided. Those who wished for a hitch-free sports event took in the two by 70 metres yet to be completed with a slight feeling of terror. All others happily pictured the juicy headlines. The following three weeks would show whether Calatrava would be right or not.

And just at the moment when the organisers intended to inform the international media that the technical miracle would be performed according to plan, the entire project had to be postponed once again. After the supporting pillars had been demounted, meticulous investigations had to be undertaken in order to assess to which extent the construction had lost its shape and whether it would still hold the load. If work continued at this pace, the stadium would have a roof right on time for the closing ceremony, an agency journalist loudly voiced his calculations. But Calatrava and his team had got their maths right: the deformations were far below the strict standards and the pulling action could commence, prompting an Athens newspaper to proclaim: *trava, trava, Calatrava!* – pull it, pull it, Calatrava…

On 5 June 2004, 13 months after the start of the construction phase and a mere two months away from the Games, the miracle was complete: the roof was positioned

1 — The Spiros Louis Stadium seen from the Athletics Centre.

2 — A weathered advertising column in the Olympic Park.

3 — The west entrance to the Olympic Park in Athens, which is open to the public.

Schlagzeilen aus. In den nächsten drei Wochen sollte sich herausstellen, ob Calatrava recht behalten würde.

Und just in dem Moment, als die internationalen Medien über den planmäßigen Beginn der technischen Hochleistung hätten informiert werden sollen, verzögerte sich die Schleppaktion erneut. Nachdem die Stützpfeiler abgebaut worden waren, musste zunächst akribisch festgestellt werden, wie stark sich die Konstruktion verformt hatte und ob sie überhaupt noch tragfähig war. Wenn es in diesem Tempo weiterginge, so rechnete ein Agenturjournalist laut nach, würde das Stadion pünktlich zur Abschlusszeremonie ein Dach haben … Doch Calatrava und sein Team hatten gut gerechnet: Die Deformationen bewegten sich weit unterhalb der strengen Normen, das Schleppen konnte beginnen. Eine Athener Zeitung titelte: *Trava, trava, Calatrava!* – Ziehe, ziehe, Calatrava!

Am 5. Juni 2004, 13 Monate nach Baubeginn und gut zwei Monate vor Beginn der Spiele, war das Mirakel geschehen: Das Dach war über dem Stadion positioniert und kurz darauf fest verankert worden. Das olympische Stadion, so frohlockte eine den internationalen Medien zugewiesene Vertreterin des Organisationskomitees «Athina 2004», würde plangemäß und rechtzeitig vor der Eröffnung fertiggestellt sein. Von wegen. Plangemäß war an diesem Tag schon lange nichts mehr in Athen. Rechtzeitig ein Fremdwort. Bautrupps buddelten, hämmerten und bohrten im 24-Stunden-Betrieb auf der größten Baustelle Griechenlands seit der Errichtung des Parthenons, zweieinhalb Jahrtausende zuvor. Seit Monaten lag die Stadt unter einer feinen Staubschicht. Die ganze Stadt fühlte sich so, wie der Langstreckenläufer Spiros Louis sich gefühlt haben mag, als er 1896 siegreich in das marmorne Panathinaiko-Stadion, Austragungsort der ersten Olympischen Spiele der Gegenwart, hineingerannt war — es ging ihr der Atem aus. Spiros Louis war der Namensgeber des olym-

4 — Das Olympiastadion «Spiros Louis» mit seiner filigranen Dachkonstruktion.

above the stadium and, shortly after, firmly fixed to the building. The Olympic stadium would be finished according to plan and right on time before the opening ceremony, a representative of the Organising Committee 'Athina 2004', who was in charge of communicating with the international media, jubilantly said. As if. By then, nothing really went 'according to plan' anymore in Athens. 'Right on time' had turned into an alien concept. Day and night worker units were digging, hammering and drilling away on the biggest Greek construction site since the erection of the Parthenon 2,500 years before. For months, the city was covered by a thin layer of dust. The entire city felt like long-distance runner Spiros Louis must have felt in 1896, when he was first to cross the finish line at the marble-built Panathenaic Stadium, the venue of the first Olympic Games of modern times – out of breath. Incidentally, Spiros Louis was the sportsman who lent his name to the Olympic

stadium in Maroussi. The president of the Organising Committee, Gianna Angelopoulos-Daskalaki, also compared the preparations to the feat of a marathon runner: Athens would have to complete a marathon at the pace of a sprinter in the preparation of the 2004 Summer Games.

At some point the critics fell silent. The arches, brightly lit by day and night, could be seen from far away. The superlative roof had added a new architectural landmark to Athens. In a city that had been spreading across the Attic landscape through the addition of chaotic, unplanned and unsightly buildings since the 1950s, this could hardly be called a luxury. A close look at daylight even forced the Cassandras to admit that Calatrava had accomplished a bold design with the Spiros Louis Stadium, the Velodrome and the Wall of Nations. The architect himself called his sketches 'classical', stating that he had been aiming for a fusion of Mediterranean spirit and homage

to Byzantine shapes. Most people had to agree that his plan had worked out rather well. There was only one point of criticism that even Calatrava was not able to negate: the fact that the roof construction alone had devoured 100 million euros seemed like a waste of almost Olympic magnitude. Money as such, however, was not yet an issue in the country swollen with Olympic euphoria.

Once the International Broadcast Centre was connected to the stadium also in terms of communications, the radio and TV stations that were housed there began to prepare for the actual Games.

At first glance, the building itself resembled a drawn-out tin box rising from the ground to the Spiros Louis Stadium like a funnel. Architect Adam Berler wanted to symbolise the connection between the stadium and the outside world: the IBC was to suck in all that was happening inside the stadium and blare it out into the world.

Essay von Werner van Gent

pischen Stadions in Maroussi. Der Vergleich mit dem Marathonläufer wurde auch von der Präsidentin des Organisationskomitees, Gianna Angelopoulos-Daskalaki, herangezogen: Athen müsse bei der Vorbereitung der Sommerspiele 2004 einen Marathonlauf im Tempo eines Schnellläufers absolvieren.

Doch allmählich verstummten die Kritiker. Aus größter Ferne waren die Tag und Nacht hell beleuchteten Bögen sichtbar. Mit dem Dach der Superlative hatte Athen einen neuen architektonischen Akzent gesetzt. Kein Luxus in einer Stadt, die sich seit den 1950er-Jahren chaotisch, planlos und hässlich in der attischen Landschaft breitgemacht hatte. Bei Lichte betrachtet mussten auch die Kassandras eingestehen: Calatrava war mit dem Spiros-Louis-Stadion, dem Velodrom und der Mauer der Nationen ein kühner Entwurf gelungen. Der Architekt selbst sagte, sein Plan sei klassisch, die Erhebungen eine Hommage an byzantinische Formen, während der Geist mediterran sei. Nicht wenige waren der Ansicht, diese Fusion sei gelungen. Doch einen Kritikpunkt konnte auch Calatrava nicht ausräumen – dass allein die Dachkonstruktion 100 Millionen Euro verschlungen hatte, mutete wie eine Verschwendung von geradezu olympischen Ausmaßen an. Noch war Geld aber kein Thema im Griechenland der olympischen Euphorie.

Nachdem das International Broadcast Centre nun auch technisch mit dem Stadion verbunden war, hatten die dort untergebrachten Radio- und Fernsehstationen begonnen, sich auf die eigentlichen Spiele vorzubereiten.

Das Gebäude selbst sah auf den ersten Blick aus wie eine lang gezogene Blechschachtel, die sich wie ein Trichter aus dem Boden zum Spiros-Louis-Stadion erhob. Architekt Adam Berler symbolisierte damit die Verbindung des Stadions mit der Außenwelt; das IBC sollte das Geschehen im Stadion aufsaugen und in die Welt hinausposaunen.

5 — Das Panathinaiko-Stadion im Stadtzentrum, als Rekonstruktion des antiken Stadions für die ersten Spiele der Neuzeit 1896 gebaut.

This special information factory also hosted the Swiss TV. On barely 100 square metres, 60 technicians, journalists and camerapeople were preparing for the broadcasting marathon. Tasks were relegated in a meeting. The correspondent, who was living in Athens at the time, was given the honourable task of commenting on the opening and closing ceremony together with sports journalist Bernhard Thurnheer. In between the two occasions, his local knowledge put him in charge of 'anything that might go wrong'. Word on the street was that this had to be a Herculean task – if anything could be agreed on in this windowless room, it was that *something* would definitely go wrong. Massive delays on almost all construction sites had jettisoned the scheduled test periods. In many places, there was not even enough time for a final rehearsal.

The meeting participants had overlooked one thing: a genuinely Greek phenomenon, which has accounted for the unpredictability of any event in this corner of the world since the times of antiquity. It is composed of an extreme form of individualism, which, in everyday life, can often turn into boundless egotism, a pride that sometimes borders on stubbornness, but can also be expressed by selfless hospitality, and the refusal to bow to the constraints of an ill-disposed environment or the insistence to resist these constraints by all available – and yet to be discovered – means.

There is a word for this phenomenon in Greek: *filotimo,* which does not translate well to other languages. The Greek gods must have chosen Friday, 13 August 2004, as the perfect day to unleash *filotimo* unto the city. Early in the morning the slightly panicky rush of the past months seemed to have died down. There were still tensions in the air, but also excitement about having made it so far. Athens could finally prove all the naysayers wrong.

4 — The Spiros Louis Stadium and its delicate roof construction.

5 — The Panathenaic Stadium in the city centre is a reconstruction of an ancient Greek stadium and was built for the first modern Olympic Games in 1896.

Im Inneren dieser Informationsfabrik der besonderen Art war auch das Schweizer Fernsehen untergebracht. Auf nicht viel mehr als 100 Quadratmetern bereiteten sich 60 Techniker, Journalisten und Kameraleute auf den Sendemarathon vor. In einer Sitzung wurden die Aufgaben verteilt. Dem in Athen ansässigen Korrespondenten wurde die großartige Aufgabe zuteil, zusammen mit Sportredakteur Bernhard Thurnheer die Eröffnungs- und die Abschlussfeier zu kommentieren. Dazwischen war er aufgrund seiner Kenntnisse der lokalen Begebenheiten zuständig «für alles, was schieflaufen sollte». Eine Herkules-Aufgabe, meinte man zu diesem Zeitpunkt noch. Denn darüber, dass vieles schieflaufen würde, war man sich im fensterlosen Raum einig. Die massiven Verspätungen auf fast allen Baustellen hatten die geplanten Testperioden aufgeschluckt. An vielen Stellen gab es nicht mal mehr genügend Zeit für eine Generalprobe.

Die Sitzungsteilnehmer hatten etwas übersehen: ein urgriechisches Phänomen, das jegliche Vorhersagen in dieser Ecke der Welt unmöglich macht, und das schon seit der Antike. Es setzt sich zusammen aus einer extremen Form des Individualismus, der im Alltag oft zu einem grenzenlosen Egoismus ausartet, einem gelegentlich störrisch wirkenden Stolz, der sich aber auch in selbstloser Gastfreundschaft äußern kann, und der Weigerung, sich den Zwängen einer nicht gerade freundlichen Umwelt zu beugen beziehungsweise sich diesen Zwängen mit allen zur Verfügung stehenden – und einigen noch zu erfindenden – Mitteln zu widersetzen.

Im Griechischen gibt es ein Wort dafür: *Filotimo*, das aber so in keine andere Sprache zu übersetzen ist. Freitag, der 13. August 2004, war von der griechischen Götterwelt als der ideale Tag erkoren worden, dieses *Filotimo* zu entfalten. Schon am frühen Morgen schien sich die panische Hektik der vergangenen Monate etwas gelegt zu haben. Spannung lag in der Luft, das schon, aber auch Freude, dass

6 – Im Olympischen Dorf, am nördlichen Stadtrand von Athen, ist das Trainingsschwimmbecken verwaist.

7 – Der Marmorspringbrunnen mit den olympischen Ringen ist stark beschädigt.

Not a single one of the predictions came true on this day or in the following 15 days: no traffic chaos hindered the approximately 70,000 spectators from reaching the Spiros Louis Stadium. No choking cloud of smog poisoned the air. Nowhere even a tang of the predicted foul mood could be detected in the demeanour of the Athenians, who are usually not overflowing with affability. The most impressive part was the army of volunteers. Had not everybody be convinced that the Greeks would never be caught doing work for free in a million years? The opposite was the case: everywhere guests from abroad were welcomed by friendly volunteers.

And there was something else that no one had dared to predict: almost a third of Athens' inhabitants had retreated to the province, the islands or their home villages to follow the Games on their television sets. The city took a deep breath. The extra lanes reserved for athletes, officials and media representatives were generally respected. Tens of thousands of colourful little flags lent the city, which laid no claim to the title of the most beautiful place in the world, a particularly festive air.

And thus began a fabulous party at the Spiros Louis Stadium on the eve of 13 August that would go on for 15 days. The opening ceremony, sometimes bordering on kitsch without giving in to it completely, was performed without any hitches. It was a homage to Greek history, mythology, but also poets of modern Greece, such as Jorgos Seferis. For three and a half hours, the fast-changing settings mesmerised the spectators in the stadium as well as a broad audience of viewers at home, as the audience ratings revealed the next day. Inevitably, in the end a showy fireworks performance rang in the beginning of the Games.

Only two days later the first scandal dampened the mood. Sprinter Katerini Thanou and her colleague Kostas Kenteris had refused a doping test on the eve of the opening ceremony and had been brought to a hospital by their coach, where they were kept out of sight from the world. Three days later they withdrew from the competition. Whether they had resorted to doping or not could never be proven, but the reproach weighed down heavily on them. Greek athletics, alas, looks back on a long and not particularly glorious history in this respect.

The potential case of cheating did not darken the mood for long, though. The party was well under way and everybody was determined to enjoy it to the fullest. The Games had turned into a national party also in a figurative way: Greece had proven to itself and the world that it could turn around even the most hopeless of situations. Comparisons were made to the classical win at Marathon almost two and a half thousand years earlier. More seldom heard was the reference to the even more dramatic victory of Athens and its allies ten years after that, in September 480 B.C., in the

man es bis hierher geschafft hatte. Jetzt konnte Athen endlich zeigen, dass die Unkenrufe fehl am Platz gewesen waren.

Nichts von all dem, was vorausgesagt worden war, traf an diesem Tag und an allen 15 darauffolgenden Tagen ein: Kein Verkehrschaos hinderte die rund 70 000 Zuschauer daran, in das Spiros-Louis-Stadion zu kommen. Keine beißende Smogwolke verpestete die Luft. Nirgends gab es auch nur einen Hauch der vorhergesagten miesen Stimmung bei den ansonsten nicht vor Freundlichkeit strotzenden Athenern. Am eindrücklichsten war die Armee von Freiwilligen. Hatte es nicht im Vorfeld geheißen, nie würden sich die Griechinnen und Griechen dazu überreden lassen, freiwillige Arbeit zu leisten? Das Gegenteil war eingetroffen: Überall begrüßten freundliche Helferinnen und Helfer die ausländischen Gäste.

Und noch etwas hatte niemand vorauszusagen gewagt: Fast ein Drittel der Einwohner Athens hatten sich in die Provinz, auf die Inseln oder in ihre Heimatdörfer zurückgezogen, um die Spiele im Fernsehen zu verfolgen. Die Stadt atmete auf. Die für die Sportler, Funktionäre und Medienleute reservierten Sonderspuren wurden allgemein respektiert. Zehntausende von farbigen Fähnlein gaben der Stadt, die für sich nicht das Prädikat beansprucht, die schönste der Welt zu sein, ein besonders feierliches Antlitz.

Und so begann am Abend des 13. August im Spiros-Louis-Stadion eine grandiose Fete, die 15 Tage lang anhalten sollte. Die Eröffnungsfeier ging reibungslos über die Bühne, streifte hie und da zwar die Grenze des Kitschigen, ohne aber lange dort zu verweilen. Der Geschichte Griechenlands, der Mythologie, aber auch Dichtern des modernen Griechenlands wie Jorgos Seferis wurde gehuldigt. Dreieinhalb Stunden lang fesselte die rasch wechselnde Szenerie die Zuschauer im Stadion und, wie die Auswertung der Einschaltquoten am nächsten Tag belegte, auch ein breites Publikum zu Hause. Am

8 — Treppe beim Westzugang des Olympiaparks mit Fußgängerpasserelle.

straits between Attica and Salamis Island. In a situation of sheer hopelessness, Themistocles and his fleet unexpectedly and gloriously defeated the overwhelmingly strong army of Persian king Xerxes.

This much glory can turn people blind. Almost 2,500 years after Marathon and Salamis, nobody in Athens was interested in the tremendous costs that this new victory had amassed. The Greek media were the only ones to show outrage at the exorbitant rise in expenditure on security.

A Swiss zeppelin wheeling above the city with a discreet hum was the most visible sign of the security measures undertaken. However, the airship did not spy a single terrorist during the two weeks of the Games, not even a thief — those had apparently also left the city. The one place where the cameras eventually spotted something was the port city of Piraeus. Two harbour police officers gave in to their desire behind a shed in what they thought was a private moment

and got caught on camera… The fallible officer and her lover, so the rumour went, were discharged from service shortly after.

A meagre success or a triumph of Greek security efforts? Everybody is entitled to their opinion. One thing can be said for sure — the issue of security was grossly inflated in the run-up to the Games. Especially US-American media had tutted at the incompetence of the poorly equipped Greek police force time and again. The Greek government had nothing much to offer in reply than to keep buying ever more expensive devices and systems.

That, of course, jacked up costs. During an interview the television crew could witness live what was happening in this respect. The head of a company specialising in metal detectors had assumed that nobody from the foreign team was proficient in the Greek language. The interview was done in English and interrupted by a short telephone call. On the other end of the line the

6 — The abandoned training pool in the Olympic Village, located at the northern fringe of Athens.

7 — The marble fountain featuring the Olympic rings is severely damaged.

8 — Stairs at the Olympic Park's west entrance and footbridge.

Ende, es musste so kommen, läutete ein pompöses Feuerwerk den Beginn der Spiele ein.

Schon zwei Tage später kam der erste Dämpfer. Die Schnellläuferin Katerini Thanou und ihr Kollege Kostas Kenteris hatten sich am Vorabend der Eröffnungsfeier einer Dopingkontrolle entzogen und waren von ihrem Trainer in ein Krankenhaus gebracht worden, wo sie hermetisch von der Außenwelt abgeriegelt wurden. Nach drei Tagen zogen sie sich aus dem Wettbewerb zurück. Ob sie gedopt waren, konnte nie nachgewiesen werden, der Vorwurf lastete aber schwer. Die griechische Leichtathletik muss diesbezüglich leider auf eine lange und nicht besonders ruhmreiche Geschichte zurückblicken.

Der mögliche Betrugsfall konnte die Stimmung nicht lange beeinträchtigen. Die Fete war in vollem Gange und man war auch fest entschlossen, sie bis zum Ende zu genießen. Auch im übertragenen Sinne waren die Spiele zu einer nationalen Fete geworden; Griechenland hatte sich und der Welt bewiesen, in einer schier aussichtslosen Situation dennoch gewinnen zu können. Vergleiche mit dem klassischen Sieg bei Marathon, fast zweieinhalbtausend Jahre zuvor, kamen zum Zuge. Seltener war der Hinweis auf den noch viel dramatischeren Sieg der Athener und ihrer Alliierten zehn Jahre später, im September 480 v. Chr. in der Meerenge zwischen Attika und der Insel Salamis. Auch dort herrschte eine schier aussichtslose Ausgangslage in der Schlacht gegen die übermächtige Streitkraft des persischen Großkönigs Xerxes, die dann aber von Themistokles und seiner Flotte unerwartet und grandios gewonnen wurde.

Soviel Ruhm macht blind. Fast zweieinhalbtausend Jahre nach Marathon und Salamis wollte in Athen niemand wissen, zu welchen immensen Kosten der neue Sieg gekauft worden war. Am ehesten noch empörten sich die griechischen Medien über den exorbitanten Anstieg der Kosten im Sicherheitsbereich.

9 — Die zeitlose Marmortribüne mit Laufbahn im Panathinaiko-Stadion.

mayor of one of the larger tourist islands in the Aegean voiced his concerns regarding the newly imposed requirement to mount pricey metal detectors around the port on top of everything else. 'Don't worry, Mister Mayor', he was reassured by the company head, 'we'll send you an invoice, you'll send us an invoice back, and everyone's happy!' The CEO mentioned the concern of the worried mayor to the interviewer after finishing his call – without disclosing the underlying financial construction, of course. Back then, reviews of expenditure were extremely sparse, allowing for millions to be misappropriated into people's pockets with such simple constructions. It is estimated that 25 per cent of the overall costs were spent this way, which would account for almost three billion euros. Eventually, costs for security, originally capped at 500 million, exceeded one billion euros. Said island, by the way, never put up any metal detectors. Only very few cases of fraud

were uncovered – probably also because nobody thought it appropriate to look for them. Back then everyone believed that the Olympic Games would bail out the Greek economy for all eternity.

Escaping this kind of euphoria was no easy thing. Athenians still go into raptures over the metro that partly resembles an underground museum. Everyone knew that the age-old dream of an underground line in Athens would never have come true without the pressure of the Olympic Games. The city's inhabitants were a little less euphoric about the reintroduced tramway line. Too slow, was the overall consensus – although that might have been due to the transport minister's adamant refusal to give the tramway right of way over cars in the heavy Athens traffic. The most sustainable investments, it seemed, were those in the new Athens International Airport, named after Eleftherios Venizelos. In terms of architectural design, the terminal was a monstrosity, having spent 15 years

in a drawer and being none the prettier for it. Compared to the two terminals of the old Ellinikon International Airport, however, the new one worked impeccably. That August of 2004, even the difficult times when the new airport could exclusively be reached from the air (as the Attiki Odos city motorway leading to the airport had not yet been completed) were forgotten.

These two victorious weeks of August presumably cost the Greek state over eleven billion euros – official figures on the actual spending were never published. Estimated costs accounted for approximately six per cent of the country's overall debt in 2004 – a hefty sum. Still it would be wrong to say that the Games were the final straw that caused one of the worst debt crises ever to befall the Greek society five years on.

In 2009, Greece's debt had already risen to approximately 300 billion euros. Kostas Karamanlis' conservative government had proceeded on the path embarked

Ein mit diskretem Brummen über der Stadt kreisender Zeppelin aus der Schweiz war das sichtbarste Zeichen dieser Sicherheitsanstrengungen. Erfasst haben die spähenden Augen des Luftschiffes in den zwei olympischen Wochen allerdings keinen Terroristen, noch nicht mal einen einzigen Dieb – auch diese hatten sich offenbar aus der Stadt verzogen. Fündig wurden die Kameras lediglich in der Hafenstadt Piräus. Dort ertappten sie zwei Angestellte der Hafenpolizei, die sich, vermeintlich unsichtbar für die Außenwelt, hinter einem Schuppen der Wonne der Lust hingaben ... Die fehlbare Polizistin und der fehlbare Polizist seien daraufhin entlassen worden.

Ein magerer Erfolg oder doch ein Triumph der griechischen Sicherheitsbestrebungen? Man kann es sehen, wie man will. Sicher ist aber, dass im Vorfeld der Spiele hoch gepokert wurde um das Thema Sicherheit. Vor allem amerikanische Medien hatten immer wieder die Unfähigkeit der schlecht ausgerüsteten griechischen Polizei herausgestrichen. Die Regierung hatte dem nicht viel anderes entgegenzusetzen, als immer teurere Geräte und Systeme einzukaufen.

Das wiederum trieb die Kosten in die Höhe. Bei einem Interview konnte das Fernsehteam live verfolgen, was sich auf diesem Gebiet abspielte. Der Leiter einer auf Metalldetektoren spezialisierten Firma hatte angenommen, dass das ausländische Team der Landessprache nicht mächtig sei. Das Interview wurde auf Englisch geführt und kurz von einem Telefonat unterbrochen. Am anderen Ende war der Bürgermeister einer größeren Tourismusinsel in der Ägäis, der offenkundig Probleme mit der neuen Auflage hatte, nun auch noch teure Metalldetektoren am Hafen aufzustellen. «Aber Herr Bürgermeister, machen Sie sich doch keine Sorgen», antwortete der Firmeninhaber, «wir stellen Ihnen eine Rechnung aus, daraufhin können Sie uns eine Gegenrechnung schicken und alle sind glücklich!» Das Anliegen des besorgten Bürgermeisters eröffnete der Firmeninhaber

10 – Ein verschlossener Zugang zum «Olympic Indoor Sports Centre».

on by his socialist predecessor Kostas Simitis to the last detail, at times even perfecting it. Truth be spoken, the country's economic policy was a continuation of the Olympic celebrations by other means. Problems, bottlenecks and conflicts were solved through ever new loans. There were hardly any checks in place. The country seemed to think that financial resources were unlimited, and what was more: creditors did not waste a lot of time enquiring. After all, the country had entered the Euro zone on 1 January 2001. Creditors and debtors thus both assumed that not much could go wrong. It all seemed like an endless game at which everybody could only win. The construction industry continued to boom on the outskirts of Athens, the islands and in the province; villas kept getting larger, as did the cars parked in front of them. Especially four-wheel-drive cars of German production – preferably in black – were popular.

Only the state kept getting poorer, as nobody seemed particu-

larly interested in adapting the tax system to the new circumstances. Concern for the state never had a strong tradition in Greece. The demon of extreme individualism had returned as well, and it was stronger than ever before. The only thing missing was *filotimo*. When disaster struck because the markets, startled at the burst real-estate bubble in the US, suddenly showed signs of alarm in Greece in 2009, politicians had no clue how to react. Kostas Karamanlis threw in the towel when he realised the hopelessness of the situation. His socialist opponent Giorgos Papandreou announced that 'there is money!' and won the elections, only to find out that money had in fact run out. When the country, thanks to European financial aid, escaped an uncontrolled bankruptcy by the skin of its teeth, Papandreou's fellow party member Theodoros Pangalos commented that 'we all ate together'. This statement earned him his share of malicious comments. Eventually,

9 – The timeless marble grandstands and running track of the Panathenaic Stadium.

10 – The entrance to the Olympic Indoor Sports Centre is closed.

dem Interviewer nach dem Telefonat. Die finanzielle Konstruktion
erwähnte er wohlweislich nicht. Eine kaum existierende Kontrolle
der Ausgaben machte es in dieser Zeit möglich, dass Millionen mit
solchen einfachen Konstruktionen zweckentfremdet in fremde
Taschen flossen. Schätzungen gehen von 25 Prozent der Gesamtkosten
aus, das wären also knapp drei Milliarden Euro. Tatsache ist, dass
die ursprünglich auf 500 Millionen bezifferten Kosten für die
Sicherheit am Ende die Milliarde überschritten hatten. Die besagte
Insel hat übrigens niemals Metalldetektoren aufgestellt. Aufge-
flogen sind nur sehr wenige Betrugsfälle, wohl auch deshalb, weil
niemand es für angemessen hielt, danach zu suchen. Noch glaubten
alle, die Olympischen Spiele würden die griechische Wirtschaft
für alle Ewigkeit gesund sanieren.

Es war schwer, sich der Euphorie zu entziehen. Richtig ins
Schwärmen geraten die Athener auch heute noch angesichts der Metro,
die stellenweise eher einem unterirdischen Museum gleicht. Allen
war klar, dass der uralte Traum einer Athener Metro ohne den Druck
der Spiele niemals hätte verwirklicht werden können. Etwas weniger
euphorisch waren die Athener angesichts der wieder eingeführten
Straßenbahnlinie. Zu langsam, lautete alsbald der Befund, was allerdings damit zusammenhing, dass der zuständige Verkehrsminister
sich energisch weigerte, der Bahn im dichten Athener Verkehr Vor-
tritt zu verleihen. Am nachhaltigsten schienen die Investitionen
für den neuen Flughafen Eleftherios Venizelos. Architektonisch
war der Terminal zwar eine Monstrosität, die anderthalb Jahrzehnte
in einer Schublade vor sich hingedämmert hatte und in dieser Zeit
nicht schöner geworden war. Verglichen mit den zwei Terminals des
alten Flughafens Ellinikon funktionierte der neue Flughafen aber
tadellos. Vergessen war im August 2004 auch die schwere Zeit, als der
neue Flughafen im Grunde nur aus der Luft zu erreichen war, weil

11 — Das olympische Beachvolleyballcenter in
Faliro. Die Vegetation breitet sich im ungenutzten
Stadion aus.

12 — Die Infrastruktur verwittert oder wird auch
durch Vandalen beschädigt.

however, history proved him right,
although the villa owners had
'eaten' much more than the low-
level civil servants, whose income
was cut in half in the course of
the subsequent crisis manage-
ment. Greece had lived far beyond
its means, having succumbed to
the erroneous assumption that the
windfall would never stop. The
country basically lived like an
oil emirate for 20 years, only
without the oil. The Olympic Games
were thus a beacon of the future.

Since 2004, the Olympic facilities have been mostly left to
themselves, resulting in their
growing dilapidation. Maintenance
would have cost the state 80 to
100 million euros annually. This
money, however, was definitely no
longer available. Only when the
desolate condition of the country's
finances became obvious did Greece
remember the Olympic gold. The
approximately 500-hectare area of
the former Ellinikon International
Airport was considered the
most valuable part among the Olympic facilities. The impressive

canoe and kayak centre, the baseball stadium, the former hangar
turned into a fencing hall and the
field hockey stadium had been
placed north and south of the two
runways. Demolishing them would
have been both too expensive
and time-consuming. Even the two
flight terminals had been left
to stand. Everyone kept saying
that later on, a master plan would
help politicians make good on
their promise that the new buildings would improve the quality
of life in Athens after the Games.
After the last Olympic event, however, the fuss about Elliniko's
sports facilities died down. When
the crisis hit, politicians tried
to sell their choice property.
Up to five billion euros could
be made in a sale, it was said initially. Shortly after, disillu-
sionment followed. By now, the
state would be lucky to make half
a billion. At the edge of the
runway, on the area of the former
American base, inhabitants of the
neighbouring municipality have
taken up planting tomatoes. One of

the shacks hosts volunteer doctors
who offer their services free of
charge in a social health centre.
During the crisis, three out of
eleven million Greeks lost social
security and thus their claim to
state-funded health insurance.

But there is a silver lining:
just as in August 2004, when nobody could believe their eyes
in light of the army of highly mo-
tivated volunteers, the Greek
society rediscovered solidarity
during the years of the crisis.

At the closing ceremony on
29 August 2004, the president of
the Organising Committee, Gianna
Angelopoulos-Daskalaki, said in
the Spiros Louis Stadium filled
with 72,000 spectators: 'The world
has discovered a new Greece — the
last gold medal of these Games
belongs to all Greeks.' Then came
a long, enduring hangover.

In 2015, eleven years after
the Games, the Greek society, heavily shaken by the financial crisis, struggles to rise once again
to come out of a situation of sheer
hopelessness as a winner.

die Stadtautobahn zum Flughafen, die Attiki Odos, noch nicht fertiggestellt war.

Die zwei siegreichen Augustwochen haben den griechischen Staat vermutlich weit über elf Milliarden Euro gekostet – offizielle Zahlen sind diesbezüglich nie veröffentlicht worden. Die geschätzten Ausgaben entsprachen 2004 rund sechs Prozent der damaligen Gesamtverschuldung. Ein happiger Betrag. Dennoch ist es falsch zu sagen, die Spiele seien ausschlaggebend gewesen für den Ausbruch einer der schlimmsten Schuldenkrisen, in welche die griechische Gesellschaft fünf Jahre später geraten sollte.

Im Jahr 2009 war die Verschuldung Griechenlands bereits auf rund 300 Milliarden Euro angestiegen. Die konservative Regierung von Kostas Karamanlis hatte die Rezeptur seines sozialistischen Vorgängers Kostas Simitis bis ins letzte Detail fortgesetzt und stellenweise noch perfektioniert. Genau genommen handelte es sich um eine Fortsetzung der olympischen Fete mit anderen Mitteln. Probleme, Engpässe und Konflikte wurden mit immer neuen Krediten gelöst. Kontrollen gab es kaum. Geld war aus griechischer Sicht unbeschränkt vorhanden und das Schönste dabei: Die Gläubiger fragten nicht lange nach. Das Land befand sich seit dem 1. Januar 2001 ja im Euroraum. Da konnte nichts schiefgehen, dachten Gläubiger und Schuldner. Es erschien im Grunde wie ein endloses Spiel, bei dem alle nur gewinnen konnten. An den Rändern Athens, auf den Inseln und in der Provinz boomte die Bauindustrie weiter, die Villen wurden größer, die davor geparkten Autos auch. Besonders beliebt waren vierradgetriebene Wagen aus deutscher Produktion, vorzugsweise in der Farbe Schwarz.

Ärmer wurde nur der Staat, weil niemand sich sonderlich dafür interessierte, das Steuersystem den Gegebenheiten anzupassen. Um den Staat hat sich in Griechenland noch niemand besonders große Sorgen gemacht. Auch der Dämon des extremen Individualismus war wieder da, stärker denn je zuvor. Was fehlte, war lediglich das *Filotimo*. Als das Desaster sich ankündigte, weil die Märkte, aufgeschreckt vom Platzen der Immobilienblase in den USA, 2009 plötzlich auch in Griechenland hellhörig wurden, reagierte die Politik ratlos. Kostas Karamanlis warf das Handtuch, als er merkte, wie aussichtslos die Lage Griechenlands geworden war. Sein sozialistischer Widersacher Giorgos Papandreou verkündete «Es gibt Geld!» und gewann damit prompt die Wahlen, nur um festzustellen, dass es eben doch kein Geld mehr gab. Als mit europäischer Hilfe ein ungeregelter Bankrott gerade noch abgewendet werden konnte, sagte Papandreous Parteifreund Theodoros Pangalos: «Wir haben es alle aufgefressen.» Damit hat er viel Häme geerntet. Doch am Ende sollte er recht behalten, auch wenn die Villenbesitzer weit mehr als die einfachen Staatsangestellten «gefressen» hatten, die im Verlauf der darauffolgenden Krisenbewältigung ihre Einkommen halbiert sahen. Griechenland hatte weit über seine Verhältnisse gelebt in der irrigen Annahme, dass der Geldregen nie aufhören würde. Im Grunde lebte das Land 20 Jahre lang wie ein Ölemirat – wenngleich ohne Öl. Die Olympischen Spiele waren so gesehen ein Fanal.

Seit 2004 hat man die olympischen Anlagen größtenteils sich selbst überlassen. Sie verlotterten zusehends. 80 bis 100 Millionen Euro hätte die jährliche Wartung verschlungen. Dieses Geld gab es aber definitiv nicht mehr. Erst als klar wurde, in welch desolatem Zustand sich die griechischen Staatsfinanzen befanden, erinnerte man sich wieder an das olympische Gold. Das rund 500 Hektar große Gelände des ehemaligen Flughafens Ellinikon galt als das Filetstück unter den olympischen Anlagen. Das eindrückliche Kanu- und Kajakcenter, das Baseballstadion, der zu einer Fechthalle umfunktionierte Hangar und das Landhockeystadion hatte man nördlich und südlich der beiden Pisten platziert – sie abzutragen hatte sich als viel zu teuer und vor allem zu zeitaufwändig erwiesen. Sogar die zwei Flugterminals hatte man stehen lassen. Später, so hieß es immer wieder, würde man in einem Masterplan schon dafür sorgen, das Versprechen

13 — Auf dem alten Flughafenareal im Süden Athens, dem «Elliniko Olympic Complex», befindet sich auch das verwaiste Kanu- und Kajakcenter.

14 — Ein künstlicher See ermöglichte die Wasserversorgung der Kanu- und Kajakanlage.

11 — The Olympic Beach Volleyball Centre in Faliro. Vegetation has spread throughout the deserted stadium.

12 — The infrastructure that has not been ruined by acts of vandalism is decaying.

13 — The deserted canoe and kayak centre is located at the Elliniko Olympic Complex on the former airport premises in the south of Athens.

14 — An artificial pond supplies water to the canoe and kayak facilities.

der Politik einzulösen. Dies besagte, dass sämtliche Bauten nach den Spielen die Lebensqualität Athens aufwerten sollten.

Doch nach dem letzten olympischen Ereignis wurde es ruhig um die Sportanlagen Ellinikos. Jetzt wurde um das Filetstück gepokert. Bis zu fünf Milliarden Euro würde der Verkauf einbringen, hieß es zunächst noch. Dann kam die Ernüchterung. Inzwischen wäre der Staat froh, eine halbe Milliarde zu generieren. Am Rande der Piste, auf dem Gebiet des ehemaligen amerikanischen Stützpunktes, pflanzen Einwohner der benachbarten Gemeinde inzwischen Tomaten an. In einer der Baracken bieten freiwillige Ärzte in einem «sozialen Gesundheitszentrum» gratis ihre Dienste an. In der Krise sind drei von insgesamt elf Millionen Griechen ausgesteuert worden und haben keinen Anspruch mehr auf die staatliche Krankenversorgung.

Das Positive dabei: Genau wie im August 2004, als niemand seinen Augen traute angesichts einer Armee von hoch motivierten Freiwilligen, hat die griechische Gesellschaft in den Jahren der Krise die Solidarität wiederentdeckt.

Bei der Abschlussfeier am 29. August 2004 sagte die Präsidentin des Organisationskomitees, Gianna Angelopoulos-Daskalaki, im mit 72 000 Zuschauern vollbesetzten Spiros-Louis-Stadion: «Die Welt hat ein neues Griechenland entdeckt, die letzte Goldmedaille dieser Spiele gehört allen Griechen.» Dann kam der lange, lange Hangover.

2015, elf Jahre nach den Spielen, versucht sich die von der Finanzkrise arg gebeutelte griechische Gesellschaft erneut aufzurappeln, um in einer schier aussichtslosen Lage doch noch als Gewinnerin dastehen zu können.

Werner van Gent, geboren 1953 in Utrecht als Sohn niederländisch-schweizerischer Eltern. Nach der Mittelschule zog er in die Schweiz, wo er an der Universität Zürich Soziologie studierte. Noch an der Uni lernte er seine Frau Amalia kennen. Nach dem Uni-Abschluss zogen beide nach Griechenland, um von dort als freischaffende Journalisten zu arbeiten. Bald schon wurde aus dem gelegentlichen Schreiben eine reguläre Korrespondententätigkeit, zunächst für schweizerische Tageszeitungen und ab 1993 regelmäßig für Radio und Fernsehen. 2004 kommentierte er die Eröffnungs- und Abschlussfeiern der Olympischen Spiele für das Schweizer Fernsehen SRF. Werner van Gent hat mehrere Bücher und ein Theaterstück geschrieben. Seit 2007 organisiert und begleitet er für treffpunktorient.ch Reisen durch sein Berichterstattungsgebiet.

Werner van Gent was born in Utrecht in 1953 to parents of Dutch and Swiss descent. He moved to Switzerland after secondary school to study Sociology at the University of Zurich. He met Amalia, his wife-to-be, while still a student. After graduation, the couple moved to Greece, where they both worked as independent reporters. The occasional writing assignment soon turned into regular correspondent work, at first for daily newspapers in Switzerland and from 1993 also for radio and TV stations. In 2004, he was the commentator of the opening and closing ceremonies of the Olympic Games for the Swiss TV broadcaster SRF. Werner van Gent is the author of several books and a play. Since 2007 he has organised and guided tours to the regions he has reported from (treffpunktorient.ch).

Velodrom
The Velodrome

Olympisches Beachvolleyballcenter in Faliro
The Olympic Beach Volleyball Centre in Faliro

«Frieden-und-Freundschaft-Stadion» in Piräus
The Peace and Friendship Stadium in Piraeus

Ungenutzte Trainingsfelder beim olympischen Beachvolleyballcenter in Faliro
Idle training courts at the Olympic Beach Volleyball Centre in Faliro

Panathinaiko-Stadion
The Panathenaic Stadium

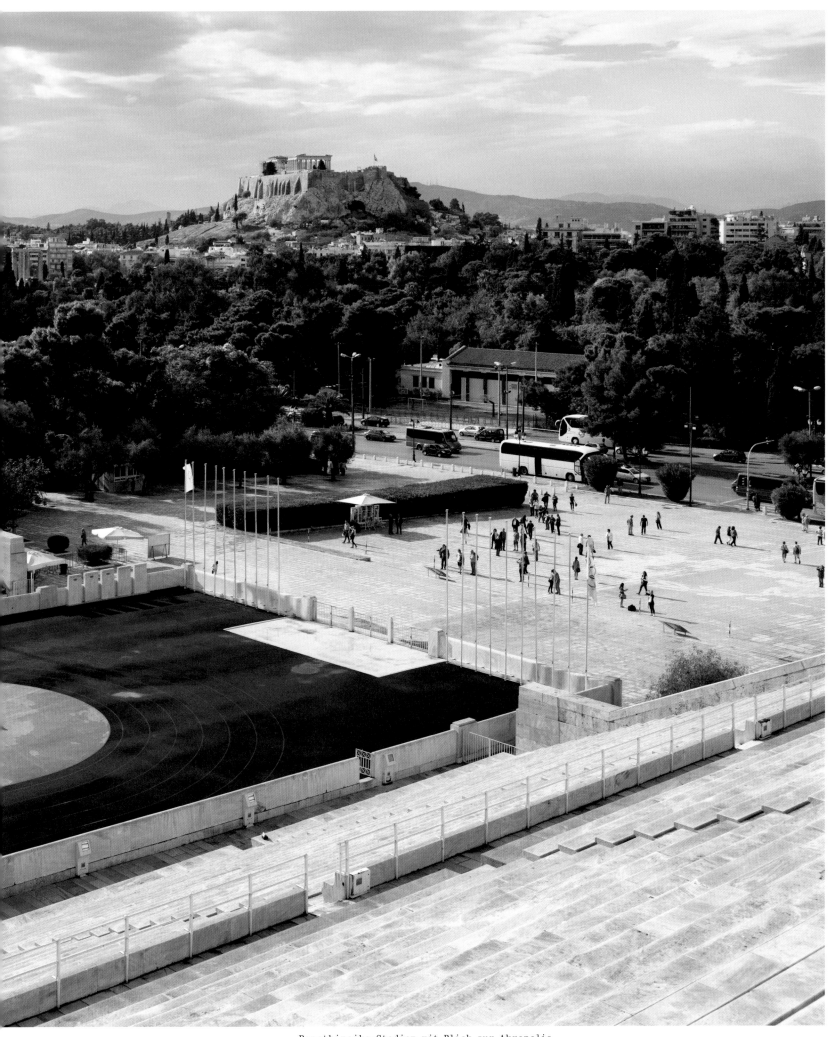

Panathinaiko-Stadion mit Blick zur Akropolis
The Panathenaic Stadium with the Acropolis in the background

Sicherheitsdienst im «Faliro Coastal Zone Olympic Sports Complex»
Security guard at the Faliro Coastal Zone Olympic Sports Complex

«Sports Pavilion», ursprünglich für Taekwondo-Wettkämpfe und Handballspiele gebaut
The Sports Pavilion, originally built for taekwondo competitions and handball games

Streunende Hunde als Begleiter im Olympiapark
In the company of stray dogs at the Olympic Park

Olympiastadion «Spiros Louis»
The Spiros Louis Stadium

Trainingsschwimmbecken und Tribüne des Schwimmstadions im Olympiapark
Training pool and grandstands of the swimming stadium in the Olympic Park

Schwimmunterricht in der großen Wassersporthalle
Swimming lessons in the grand indoor pool

Wasserkanal im Kanu- und Kajakcenter in Elliniko
Water channel at the canoe and kayak centre in Elliniko

Zugang zum Olympischen Dorf im Norden Athens
Entrance to the Olympic Village in the north of Athens

Zuschauertribüne des Kanu- und Kajakcenters in Elliniko
Grandstands at the canoe and kayak centre in Elliniko

Sitzbänke in Ringform auf dem abgesperrten «Elliniko Olympic Complex»
Circle-shaped benches at the closed Elliniko Olympic Complex

Softballstadion in Elliniko
The softball stadium in Elliniko

Softballstadion in Elliniko
The softball stadium in Elliniko

BERLIN 1936
OLYMPISCHE SOMMERSPIELE
—————————————

Die deutsche Wehrmacht grüßt
ihre Gäste

Essay von Peter Dittmann

BERLIN 1936
SUMMER OLYMPICS
—————————————

The German Wehrmacht Welcomes
Its Guests

Essay by Peter Dittmann

Reichssportfeld

Nächste Haltestelle: Olympiastadion. Etwa zehn Kilometer vom Brandenburger Tor entfernt, im Westen Berlins, liegt das Herz der Olympischen Spiele 1936. Bereits damals war es hervorragend an das Berliner Nahverkehrsnetz angeschlossen. Lediglich die U-Bahn-Station heißt heute nicht mehr Reichssportfeld, wie das Gelände von den Nationalsozialisten getauft wurde.

Auf dem kurzen Spaziergang zum Stadion geht es bergauf durch ein kleines Waldstück. Die olympischen Sportstätten befinden sich auf einer Anhöhe. Der Fußweg führt über den für die Spiele angelegten riesigen Parkplatz, da erscheint es düster, groß und mächtig, das Berliner Olympiastadion. Streng pfeift der Wind. Nur bei Fußball-Bundesligapartien von Hertha BSC drängen sich hier die Menschen und trinken vor Anpfiff ein letztes günstiges Bier an einem der improvisierten Stände, um sich etwas zu wärmen.

Zu den Spielen 1936 war der Olympische Platz vor dem Stadion mehr als ein simpler Vorplatz. Er war der letzte Abschnitt der «Via Triumphalis», der Straße des Triumphes, die vom Alexanderplatz aus quer durch Berlin verlief. Die Strecke schmückten Hakenkreuzfähnchen, feiernde Passanten schlenderten auf und ab, eine Fanmeile. Sie war ein wichtiger Baustein der nationalsozialistischen Inszenierung. Zur Eröffnungsfeier liess sich Adolf Hitler am 1. August 1936 in seinem Wagen mit offenem Verdeck die «Via Triumphalis» hinab am Lustgarten vorbei, durch das Brandenburger Tor, den Tiergarten und Charlottenburg zum Olympiastadion fahren. Entlang der prächtig dekorierten Straße drängten sich Tausende Anhänger, die dem Führer auf der Fahrt zum Reichssportfeld begeistert zujubelten.

Das olympische Protokoll verbot eine Rede Hitlers im Stadion. Dennoch wussten die Nationalsozialisten die Eröffnungszeremonie

1 — Blick über das ehemalige «Reichssportfeld», heute «Olympiapark Berlin», vom Glockenturm aus gesehen.

Reichssportfeld

Next stop: Olympiastadion. Approximately ten kilometres from the Brandenburg Gate, in the western part of Berlin, lies the heart of the 1936 Olympic Games. Even back then the venue had an excellent connection to the Berlin local public transport network. The only difference today: the underground station is no longer called Reichssportfeld, the name it was given by the National Socialists.

The short walk to the stadium leads uphill through a small wood. The Olympic sports facilities are situated atop an elevation. After a walk across the gigantic parking lot, specifically built for the Games, the Berlin Olympic stadium comes into sight – gloomy, large and mighty. The wind is howling. Today Bundesliga football matches of Hertha BSC are the one thing that has people crowding around the improvised stalls, downing a last cheap beer to warm up before kick-off.

During the 1936 Games, the Olympischer Platz in front of the stadium was more than just a simple forecourt. It was the last section of the 'via triumphalis', the triumphal way, which ran across all of Berlin, starting at Alexanderplatz. Celebrating passers-by strolled along the swastika-festooned road (what today would be called a fan park), which served as an integral part of National Socialist staging. For the opening celebrations on 1 August 1936, Adolf Hitler rode down the 'via triumphalis' in an open-top car, past the Lustgarten, the Brandenburg Gate, the zoo, and through Charlottenburg, until he reached the Olympic stadium. Thousands of followers huddled on the resplendently decorated street, cheering on the Führer on his drive to the Reichssportfeld.

Due to Olympic protocol, Hitler was not allowed to deliver a speech in the stadium. Nonetheless, the National Socialists knew how to arrange the opening

ceremony according to their wishes. A determined Hitler marched through the Marathontor (Marathon Gate) into the full Olympic stadium, while a fanfare by Richard Wagner was playing. When he arrived, the German guests in the stadium stroke up the first stanza of the Deutschlandlied, followed by the Horst Wessel song, the party hymn of the NSDAP. In the grey of the Berlin Olympic stadium, which can make you feel small and lost even today, 100,000 individuals united to form a community, and Hitler, the Führer, became absorbed by the mass of spectators.

When the US team refused to do the Nazi salute during their entry into the stadium, it was met by a deafening cascade of catcalls. This unsportsmanlike gesture, not usually encountered at Olympic Games, was a surprisingly clear indication of the political climate in fascist Germany. The audience's calls showed unequivocally that the ideas of understanding among nations and

Essay von Peter Dittmann

ganz in ihrem Sinne zu gestalten. Unterlegt von einer Fanfare Richard Wagners marschierte Hitler entschlossenen Schrittes durch das Marathontor in das vollbesetzte Olympiastadion ein. Sobald er dort angekommen war, stimmten die deutschen Stadiongäste gemeinsam die erste Strophe des Deutschlandliedes und im Anschluss das Horst-Wessel-Lied, die Parteihymne der NSDAP, an. Im Grau des Berliner Olympiastadions, in dem man sich noch heute klein und verloren fühlt, entstand aus 100 000 Individuen eine Gemeinschaft, und der Führer Hitler wurde ein Teil der Zuschauermasse.

Als das US-amerikanische Team beim Einlauf ins Stadion den Hitlergruß verweigerte, wurde es gnadenlos ausgebuht. Diese unsportliche, für Olympische Spiele ungewöhnliche Geste war ein überraschend deutlicher Hinweis auf das politische Klima im faschistischen Deutschland. Die Pfiffe des Publikums zeigten, dass die Idee der Völkerverständigung und des Weltfriedens nicht ins Weltbild der Nationalsozialisten passte. Vor der Machtergreifung war Hitler zunächst ein strikter Gegner der Ausrichtung Olympischer Spiele gewesen. Berlin hatte den Zuschlag noch während der Weimarer Republik erhalten. Als ihm die Olympischen Spiele aber unerwartet in den Schoss gefallen waren, erkannte er schnell das ungeheure innen- wie außenpolitische Potenzial.

Nicht nur im Stadion selbst, auch hinter dem 300 Meter langen, von 136 Pfeilern umgebenen Oval ist das Pathos der Spiele noch zu spüren. Hier liegt das Maifeld, das in seinen Aumaßen das Olympiastadion sogar übertrifft. Die breite, weitläufige Tribüne, welche das Feld begrenzt, wurde Westwall getauft. Diesen militärischen Begriff verwendeten die Nationalsozialisten später auch für das militärische Verteidigungssystem, das mit seinen Bunkern, Gräben und Panzersperren über 630 Kilometer hinweg die Westgrenze des Deutschen Reiches absicherte. In der Mitte des Westwalls thront der

2 — Der Haupteingang zum Olympiastadion Berlin.

world peace did not fit Nazi ideology. Before he seized power, Hitler had been strictly opposed to hosting the Summer Olympics. Berlin had won the bid during the Weimar Republic. After the Olympic Games had dropped into his lap unexpectedly, however, Hitler soon realised their immense political potential both inside the country and internationally.

The stadium itself, this 300-metre-wide oval encompassed by 136 pillars, is not the only place where one can feel the pathos of the Games. It can also be sensed on the field behind the stadium, the Maifeld, which even exceeds the Olympic stadium in its vastness. The wide, extensive stands that surround the field were called Westwall. Later on, the National Socialists also used this military term for their defence system, which secured the 630 kilometres of the western border of the German Reich with bunkers, trenches and tank traps. In the centre of the Westwall towers the 76-metre-high,

all-commanding belfry. Back then called Führerturm, it was designed to remind people of Hitler's role as leader above everyone else. At the same time, it served as a surveillance point for the security guards.

The tower's pedestal, integrated into the Westwall, hosts the Langemarckhalle, which added an explicitly nationalist character to the mega event. The hall inside the grandstand was named after the Battle of Langemarck in World War I, during which countless young German war volunteers were killed. In the Weimar Republic, gymnastic associations with a nationalist character (so-called Turnerschaften) and student associations regularly organised commemorations to honour the young men who lost their lives in this battle. The Nazis exploited the Langemarck myth as the perfect opportunity to link sports to soldiers' willingness to sacrifice themselves. After all, mass sports were first and fore-

1 — View across the former Reichssportfeld, today's Olympiapark Berlin, from the belfry.

2 — The main entrance to the Olympic stadium in Berlin.

76 Meter hohe, alles überragende Glockenturm. Damals Führerturm genannt, erinnerte er bewusst an Hitlers stets über allem stehende Rolle. Gleichzeitig diente er den Ordnungskräften dazu, das Olympiagelände zu überwachen.

Im Sockel des Turms, integriert in den Westwall, befindet sich die Langemarckhalle, in der dem sportlichen Großereignis ein explizit nationalistischer Charakter verpasst wurde. Die Halle im Inneren der Tribüne ist nach der Schlacht bei Langemarck im 1. Weltkrieg benannt, in der eine Vielzahl junger deutscher Kriegsfreiwilliger gefallen war. Während der Weimarer Republik organisierten Turnerschaften und Studentenverbindungen regelmäßig Gedenkfeiern zu Ehren der dort verstorbenen jungen Männer. Die Nationalsozialisten machten sich diesen Langemarck-Mythos zunutze, war es doch eine passende Gelegenheit, sportliche Betätigung mit militärischer Opferbereitschaft zu verknüpfen. Im Breitensport sah man ohnehin in erster Linie eine Wehrersatzübung.

Aufgrund von Einsturzgefahr wurden Glockenturm und Langemarckhalle zwei Jahre nach Kriegsende gesprengt. Trotz ihrer eindeutig nationalsozialistischen Propagandafunktion errichtete die Bundesrepublik sie zu Beginn der 60er-Jahre nach den alten Plänen wieder. Auch heute steht der kriegsverherrlichende Charakter der Anlage einer Nutzung nicht im Wege. Berührungsängste bestehen nicht, in Kürze soll das deutsche Sportmuseum hier einziehen.

Die Waldbühne direkt hinter dem Westwall ist mit ihren halbrunden Tribünen Berlins beliebteste Freilichtbühne. Hier traten schon Stars wie Bob Marley und die Rolling Stones auf. Die Arena wurde für die Olympischen Spiele 1936 errichtet und hieß zunächst Dietrich-Eckart-Freilichtbühne, benannt nach einem nationalsozialistischen Vordenker und Mentor Hitlers. Hier fanden neben den Turnwettbewerben während der Spiele auch Aufführungen völkischer

3 – Zugang zur Langemarckhalle im wieder aufgebauten Glockenturm.

most regarded as a mere stand-in for military training.

Due to the risk of collapse, both the belfry and the Langemarckhalle were demolished two years after the end of the war. Despite their unambiguous function as National Socialist propaganda, the Federal Republic re-erected them according to the old plans at the beginning of the 1960s. Even today, the war-glorifying character of the facility does not seem to hinder its further usage. Quite the opposite: the site will soon be the new home of the German sports museum, an organisation which clearly has no reserves about moving in.

The 'Waldbühne' directly behind the Westwall with its half-round stands is Berlin's most popular open-air stage. Stars like Bob Marley and the Rolling Stones have performed here. The arena was built for the 1936 Summer Olympics and was initially named after Dietrich Eckart, a Nazi 'pioneer' and Hitler's mentor. Apart from gymnastics competi-

tions, the stage also hosted performances of 'völkisch' – nationalist – plays during the Games. The facility was designed to remind people of a Germanic place of worship.

At the Olympic throwing facility, an inconspicuous small road, the Gretel-Bergmann-Weg, forks off from the footpath leading from the 'Waldbühne' to the swimming stadium. In August 2014, this path was named after an outstanding Jewish track and field athlete who was refused participation in the Summer Olympics. Gretel Bergmann, then the top German high jumper, was not nominated to participate in the Games due to 'insufficient performance' – a threadbare justification, as she had just broken the German high jump record a month before the beginning of the Games.

Gretel Bergmann symbolises the fate of all athletes who were banned from participating in the 1936 Summer Olympics. The exclusion of Jewish athletes from

the competition by the National Socialists was systematic. For the most part, they did not directly use suspension. Instead, they had been methodically excluding Jewish athletes from the sports clubs since 1933, robbing them of the possibility to train and thus reach the performance level necessary to compete in the Olympic Games.

The persecution of Jews and dissidents in Germany had prompted calls for a boycott of the Games even before they started. The International Olympic Committee (IOC), however, pleaded the principle of non-intervention in this matter, stating that it was up to Germany to nominate Jewish athletes. On an international level, Nazi Germany promised to admit Jewish athletes in return – in stark contrast to the national practice.

Only Helene Meyer, a 'half-Jew' according to the 1935 Nuremberg Laws, was nominated for the Berlin Games. The fencer fulfilled an alibi function, showcasing that in principle, Jewish-

Stücke statt. Die Anlage sollte an eine germanische Kultstätte
erinnern.

Auf dem Fußweg von der Waldbühne zum Schwimmstadion zweigt am
olympischen Wurfplatz eine unauffällige kleine Querstraße ab,
der Gretel-Bergmann-Weg. Er ist seit August 2014 nach einer herausragenden jüdischen Leichtathletin benannt, der die Teilnahme an
den Olympischen Spielen verwehrt wurde. Gretel Bergmann, damals
die beste deutsche Hochspringerin, wurde nicht für die Wettkämpfe
nominiert, mit der Begründung, ihre Leistungen seien ungenügend.
Ein fadenscheiniger Vorwand, denn einen Monat vor den Spielen hatte
sie den deutschen Rekord im Hochsprung gebrochen.

Das Schicksal Gretel Bergmanns steht sinnbildlich für die aus-
geschlossenen Sportler der Olympischen Spiele 1936. Die Nationalsozialisten grenzten jüdische Sportler systematisch von der Teilnahme an den Wettkämpfen aus. Dies geschah größtenteils nicht
direkt durch Startverbote. Vielmehr wurden jüdische Athleten seit
1933 aus den Sportvereinen ausgeschlossen und ihnen so die Möglichkeiten zum Training genommen, um das entsprechende Leistungsniveau
für Olympische Spiele zu erreichen.

Die Verfolgung von Juden und Andersdenkenden in Deutschland
hatte bereits im Vorfeld der Spiele zu Boykottaufrufen geführt.
Das Internationale Olympische Komitee (IOC) zog sich in dieser Angelegenheit jedoch auf das Prinzip der Nichteinmischung zurück.
Es sei Deutschlands Sache, jüdische Sportlerinnen und Sportler zu
nominieren. Auf internationaler Ebene versprach das nationalsozia-
listische Deutschland im Gegenzug, jüdische Sportler zu den Wettkämpfen zuzulassen, im krassen Widerspruch zur nationalen Praxis.

Zu den Spielen in Berlin wurde lediglich Helene Meyer, nach den
Nürnberger Rassegesetzen von 1935 als «Halbjüdin» bezeichnet,
nominiert. Der Fechterin kam eine Alibifunktion zu, war es doch ihre

4 — Das Eingangsportal zur ehemaligen «Dietrich-
Eckart-Freilichtbühne», die nach dem 2. Weltkrieg
zur «Waldbühne» umgebaut wurde.

German athletes could participate
in the Games. Other steps accom-
panied this gesture of tokenism.
For the duration of the Games, the
City of Berlin took down anti-
Semitic signs denying Jews access
to public buildings. Anti-Jewish
agitation articles in National
Socialist newspapers were prohib-
ited during the Olympics and the
German broadcasting companies
were admonished to stop playing
marches.

If you follow the Gretel-Bergmann-Weg a few metres to the east,
you will soon see the Olympic
swimming stadium. Its monumental
grey pillars echo the architectural design of its big brother,
the Olympic stadium. Between the
steep stands you can see swimmers
jump off the edge of the pool.
What used to host 18,000 spectators during the Olympic Games
is nowadays a public pool from May
to September. In 1936, the swimming stadium with its 50-metre
pool and 10-metre diving tower was
more than just the site of breathtaking competitions. Leni Riefen-

stahl used the Olympic pool to
shoot one of the first underwater
films.

The 1936 Summer Olympics mark
a milestone in the history of
sports event broadcasting, sur-
passing all other media events
that had taken place before it.
For the first time ever, the radio
broadcasts in 41 countries were
complemented by TV broadcasts of
the competition, making it possible to view the 175 competitions
live from outside the stadiums.
This development significantly
enhanced the national and international reach of the Olympic
Games. The broadcast in sound and
vision enabled viewers outside
the stadium to experience the
excitement of the competition at
first hand. Thanks to live television, people could witness
world records and medals being
won. At the same time, the host
nation conveyed an image of
impeccable organisation and
athleticism to the international
audience.

3 — Entrance to the Langemarckhalle inside the
reconstructed belfry.

4 — The entrance gate to the former Dietrich
Eckart amphitheatre, which was converted into
the Waldbühne after World War II.

Rolle zu verdeutlichen, dass jüdische deutsche Sportler prinzipiell teilnehmen konnten. Flankiert wurde diese beschwichtigende Maßnahme von weiteren Aktionen. Die Stadt Berlin montierte zu den Spielen antisemitische Schilder ab, die Juden den Zutritt zu öffentlichen Gebäuden untersagten. Antijüdische Hetzartikel in den nationalsozialistischen Zeitungen waren für die Zeit der Spiele untersagt, die deutschen Rundfunkstationen sollten auf Marschmusik verzichten.

Vom Gretel-Bergmann-Weg aus ein paar Meter weiter Richtung Osten erblickt man bald das olympische Schwimmstadion. Mit seinen grauen, monumentalen Säulen ist es architektonisch an seinen großen Nachbarn, das Olympiastadion, angelehnt. Zwischen den steilen Tribünen kann man Badegäste vom Beckenrand aus ins kühle Nass springen sehen. Wo zu den Olympischen Spielen noch 18 000 Zuschauer Platz fanden, herrscht heute von Mai bis September öffentlicher Badebetrieb. 1936 war das Schwimmstadion mit seinem 50-Meter-Becken und dem 10-Meter-Sprungturm mehr als ein Schauplatz atemberaubender Wettbewerbe. Im olympischen Becken filmte Leni Riefenstahl mit einer der ersten Unterwasserkameras.

Die Olympischen Spiele 1936 stellen bis heute einen Meilenstein in der Übertragung von Sportveranstaltungen dar. Sie waren ein alles Bisherige überragendes Medienereignis. So gab es neben den Radioübertragungen in 41 Länder erstmals auch Fernsehmitschnitte von den Wettbewerben. Zum ersten Mal war es möglich, auch ausserhalb der Stadien die 175 Wettkämpfe live mitzuverfolgen. Ein Umstand, der die nationale wie internationale Wirkung der Olympischen Spiele deutlich verstärkte. Erst die Übertragung in Bild und Ton ermöglichte es, auch ausserhalb des Stadions die Spannung der Wettkämpfe direkt mitzuerleben. Das Fernsehen liess die Zuschauer unmittelbar an Weltrekorden und Medaillengewinnen teilhaben.

5 — Das olympische Schwimmstadion, von Kriegsschäden verschont, besteht noch heute in seiner ursprünglichen Form.

Rowing course Berlin-Grünau

Even though the swimming stadium is located directly on the Reichssportfeld, most water competitions took place outside the central Olympic area. Sailing competitions were held in Kiel and the Olympic rowing and canoe course was situated in Grünau, a neighbourhood in the eastern part of Berlin. Here, almost 30 kilometres from the Olympic stadium, far away from the city centre, you'll find yourself in a completely different world. The whole town, marked by villas and country homes, is peaceful and green.

The impressive regatta grandstand, seating 9,000 spectators and lined with oaks and birches, is set on the bank of the Dahme. The stand was erected in 1936 for the rowing and canoe competitions. Recently a small note was put up in a display case next to the stand, advertising the return of the Olympic Games to Berlin. The first official regatta took place here as early as 1880.

For the Summer Olympics, the course just had to be deepened and widened. Next to the big stand, an additional, temporary water stand was built in 1936, allowing a total of 20,000 visitors to watch the competitions. Observed by this audience the German Olympic eight, led by coxswain Wilhelm Mahlow, won bronze in a breathtaking final round, reaching the finish in third place after the US and Italy amidst the deafening cheers of the audience. The race could have ended differently, though, given that it was strongly affected by the wind, offering the Americans rowing closer to the shore a small advantage. The first three boats reached the finish less than a second apart.

Surprisingly, the German eight that participated in the 1936 Summer Olympics were not a national squad of the best German rowers. During qualification, the club team of Wiking Berlin beat the cross-club national Olympic team and won the right to participate in the Games, which came as a

complete surprise. Under the Nazi regime, regular sports clubs were not eliminated, as opposed to workers' and confessional sports clubs. However, the political leaders wanted a selection of the best Germans to enter the Olympic rowing and canoe competitions. The athletes were supposed to identify with the German nation and the Aryan race, not their sports clubs. The bronze medal that the Wiking Berlin rowers won was thus not only a prestigious win for the German Reich, but also a small stain on the overall National Socialist staging of the Olympic Games.

The Olympic Village of Elstal

While the Wiking Berlin rowers competed right on their doorstep, the other athletes had to travel farther. Together, they lived in the Olympic Village. To pay a visit to their quarters, you have to cross the city borders. The small town of Elstal is situated a few kilometres west of Berlin in

Gleichzeitig konnte sich die Welt ein Bild von der perfekt organisierten, sportfreundlichen Gastgebernation machen.

Ruderstrecke Berlin-Grünau

Auch wenn das Schwimmstadion auf dem Reichssportfeld liegt, fanden
die Wettkämpfe zu Wasser größtenteils ausserhalb des zentralen
Olympiageländes statt. Die Segelwettbewerbe wurden in Kiel veran-
staltet, die olympische Ruder- und Kanustrecke war am östlichen
Rand Berlins, rund 30 Kilometer vom Olympiastadion entfernt, behei-
matet. Hier in Grünau, fernab des Stadtzentrums, ist man noch heute
in einer anderen Welt. Es ist friedlich und grün, Villen und Land-
häuser zeichnen das Ortsbild.

Am Ufer der Dahme liegt, gesäumt von Eichen und Birken, eine
beeindruckende, 9000 Zuschauer fassende Regattatribüne. Sie wurde
für die Ruder- und Kanuwettbewerbe 1936 errichtet. Seit kurzem
wirbt ein kleiner Zettel in einem Schaukasten neben der Tribüne
dafür, dass die Olympischen Spiele wieder nach Berlin kommen.

Die erste offizielle Regatta fand hier bereits 1880 statt. Für
die Olympischen Spiele wurde die Strecke lediglich vertieft und
verbreitert. Neben der großen Regattatribüne wurde 1936 zudem eine
temporäre Wassertribüne errichtet. So konnten insgesamt 20 000
Besucher die Wettkämpfe mitverfolgen. Vor diesem Publikum gewann
der deutsche Olympia-Achter mit Steuermann Wilhelm Mahlow in
einem atemberaubenden Endlauf unter den ohrenbetäubenden Anfeue-
rungen des Publikums hinter den USA und Italien die Bronzemedaille.
Das Rennen hätte auch einen anderen Sieger finden können, denn der
Wettkampf war stark vom Wind beeinflusst, der den näher am Ufer
rudernden Amerikanern einen kleinen Vorteil bot. Im Ziel trennte
die ersten drei Boote weniger als eine Sekunde.

6 — Peter Mahlow, Sohn von Wilhelm Mahlow,
dem Steuermann des deutschen Ruder-Achters
von 1936, auf der Tribüne der Ruderstrecke
Berlin-Grünau.

the so-called 'bacon belt' (afflu-
ent exurbs). It was built around
a railway yard about a hundred
years ago. During recent years,
the once sleepy little town with
its typical railworkers' houses
has turned into a popular destination for weekend trips for many
Berliners.

Situated along the federal
highway to Hamburg is Karl's
strawberry adventure land, featuring a potato-sack slide and
children's farm. Busloads of bar-
gain hunters on the lookout for
Armani jeans and Prada purses are
drawn to the rather kitschy,
medieval-style town centre that
was built in 2005. The area of the
Olympic Village, however, has
been attracting more and more
visitors as well. Almost ten years
ago, the Deutsche Kreditbank
foundation took over the increasingly dilapidated athletes' quarters and began to renovate the
buildings. The area has been open
to visitors since 2006. During
the 1936 Summer Olympics, almost
4,000 male athletes from 49 par-

ticipating countries lived here.
Approximately 300 female athletes
were hosted close to the Olympic
stadium, directly on the area of
the Reichssportfeld.

Today, the Olympic villages
have become an integral part
of the application concepts for
Summer and Winter Games. Organisers often praise the athletes'
quarters as an important urban
measure in the fight against
housing shortage. Sustainable investments are raised as an argument to convince the people
living close to the venue of the
Games' long-term benefit. The
idea of reusing the sites, however,
is not new.

The Olympic Village of Elstal
was not just built for the 1936
Games either. The Reichswehramt,
which acted as the contractor,
planned for the future use of the
Village from the beginning. After
the Olympic Games had ended, the
infantry training regiment of the
German Wehrmacht used the quarters for their barracks. The centre of the Village, the Speisehaus

5 — The Olympic swimming stadium suffered
no damage during the war and has survived in
its original form to this day.

6 — Peter Mahlow, son of Wilhelm Mahlow, the
coxswain of the German Olympic eight in
1936, on the grandstands of the rowing course
Berlin-Grünau.

Der deutsche Achter, der an den Olympischen Spielen 1936 teilnahm, war erstaunlicherweise keine nationale Kadermannschaft der besten deutschen Ruderer. Völlig überraschend setzte sich das Vereinsteam von Wiking Berlin in den Ausscheidungsrennen gegen die vereinsübergreifenden nationalen Olympiaauswahlen durch und durfte bei den Spielen antreten. Der Vereinssport bestand unter den Nationalsozialisten zwar fort und wurde, im Gegensatz zum Arbeiter- und zum konfessionellen Sport, nicht zerschlagen, dennoch war es der Wunsch der politischen Führung, bei den Olympischen Spielen auch in den Ruder- und Kanuwettbewerben eine zusammengestellte Auswahl der besten Deutschen antreten zu lassen. Die Sportler sollten sich über die deutsche Nation und die arische Rasse identifizieren, nicht über ihren Sportclub. So war die Bronzemedaille der Ruderer von Wiking Berlin nicht nur ein prestigeträchtiger Medaillengewinn für das Deutsche Reich, sondern zugleich auch ein kleiner Makel im Gesamtbild der nationalsozialistischen Inszenierung der Olympischen Spiele.

Das Olympische Dorf Elstal

Während die Ruderer von Wiking Berlin vor der eigenen Haustüre zu den Wettkämpfen antraten, mussten die übrigen Olympiateilnehmer einen weiteren Weg auf sich nehmen. Sie wohnten gemeinsam im Olympischen Dorf. Wer die Unterkünfte besuchen will, muss die Stadtgrenze hinter sich lassen. Einige Kilometer westlich von Berlin, im sogenannten Speckgürtel, liegt das Örtchen Elstal, das vor etwa 100 Jahren rund um einen Rangierbahnhof angelegt wurde. Aus dem verschlafenen Dorf mit seinen Eisenbahnerhäusern ist seit einigen Jahren ein beliebtes Wochenendziel vieler Hauptstädter geworden.

Direkt an der Bundesstraße nach Hamburg lockt zum einen Karls Erdbeer-Erlebnisland mit Kartoffelsack-Rutsche und Kinder-Bauern-

7 — Von den Athletenunterkünften im Olympischen Dorf Elstal ist zum Teil nur noch das Fundament zu erkennen.

8 — Die Turnhalle auf dem Areal ist in guten Zustand und dient heute als Ausstellungsraum.

der Nationen (restaurant of the nations) was remodelled as a military hospital. From the beginning of the Games participants were greeted in their quarters by posters saying 'The German Wehrmacht Welcomes Its Guests' — an ambiguous welcome that was met with criticism in the international press.

The Olympic quarters continued to be an eventful site after the end of the war. Initially, they hosted refugees from the East, who were joined by Soviet soldiers starting in 1947. The individual buildings met new purposes yet again. The Speisehaus der Nationen that had served as a military hospital to the Wehrmacht was turned into a military academy and, later on, a training centre of the Soviet Army's sports club. From the mid-70s, the Red Army demolished some of the Olympic quarters due to a lack of space. In 1983, 'Plattenbauten' — prefabricated apartment blocks — were erected in their place. They were inhabited by military staff who were assigned to control the nuclear SS-20 Saber, a type of medium-range missile.

The Soviet Army left the area in the autumn of 1991. During the following years, an investor was sought who might develop the area for housing purposes. As nobody seemed prepared to assume the considerable financial risk this entailed, the Village was used for putting jobless people to work in the 1990s. People who were unemployed during the years of German reunification had to carry out clean-up and also renovation work on the grounds. Many of the solidly built houses had become derelict over the years, despite the almost uninterrupted military use of the area.

If you take a walk across the area today expecting to feel the suffocating rigour of military barracks, you might be in for a surprise: the idyllic set-up of the Olympic Village is remarkable. Compared to the monumental Reichssportfeld, the design of the buildings in the Village is perceivably more modest. The winding footpaths and one-storey quarters fit into the landscape quite beautifully.

If you walk a few steps downhill from the partly renovated swimming stadium, you will reach a lovely birch wood. This is where Leni Riefenstahl set the beginning of 'Festival of Beauty', the second part of her film 'Olympia'. The opening scene shows a group of athletes in the morning dew, running through a little wood populated by local wildlife. In the following scene, the brawny athletes are sitting naked in the Finnish sauna of the Olympic Village, massaging their arms and legs. Sweating profusely, they are whipping their backs with twigs, sprinting from the wooden hut and jumping elegantly into the close pond. Slowly the camera glides over the wet, muscular male bodies. The seemingly perfect athletic bodies radiate discipline, strength and dynamics. Riefenstahl shows ideal humans, heroes that bear no resemblance to the average person.

hof. Zum anderen zieht es Busladungen von Schnäppchenjägern auf der Suche nach Armani-Jeans und Prada-Handtaschen in ein 2005 errichtetes mittelalterlich-kitschiges Stadtzentrum. Doch auch auf dem Gelände des Olympischen Dorfes finden sich immer mehr Interessierte ein. Vor gut zehn Jahren hat die Stiftung der DKB die Verantwortung für die zunehmend verfallenden Sportlerunterkünfte übernommen und begonnen, Gebäude zu restaurieren. Seit 2006 ist das Gelände für Besucher geöffnet. Während der Sommerspiele 1936 waren hier rund 4000 männliche Sportler aus 49 Teilnehmerländern untergebracht. Die etwa 300 Athletinnen wohnten hingegen in der Nähe des Olympiastadions, direkt auf dem Reichssportfeld.

Inzwischen sind die Olympischen Dörfer ein Kernbestandteil der Bewerbungskonzepte für Sommer- und Winterspiele. Von den Organisatoren werden die zu errichtenden Athletenunterkünfte gerne als wichtige städtebauliche Maßnahme im Kampf gegen den Wohnungsmangel angepriesen. Das Argument nachhaltiger Investitionen soll die Menschen am Ausrichtungsort von einem langfristigen Nutzen der Spiele überzeugen. Die Idee einer Nachnutzung ist jedoch gar nicht so neu.

Auch das Olympische Dorf in Elstal wurde nicht nur für die Spiele 1936 errichtet. Das Reichswehramt als Bauherr hatte den künftigen Verwendungszweck des Dorfes von Anfang an fest im Blick. Nach dem Ende der Olympischen Wettkämpfe benutzte das Infanterielehrregiment der Wehrmacht die Unterkünfte als Kaserne. Der Mittelpunkt des Dorfes, das Speisehaus der Nationen, wurde zum Militärkrankenhaus umgebaut. Bereits zu den Spielen empfingen Plakate mit der Aufschrift «Die deutsche Wehrmacht grüßt ihre Gäste» die Olympiateilnehmer in ihren Unterkünften, ein zweideutiges Willkommen, das in der internationalen Presse für Kritik sorgte.

Die olympischen Unterkünfte durchlebten auch nach Kriegsende eine abwechslungsreiche Geschichte. Zunächst kamen hier Flüchtlinge

9 — Die Schwimmhalle während Renovationsarbeiten im Jahr 2012.

10 — 1947 wurden große Teile des Olympischen Dorfes von der Sowjetischen Armee bezogen und bis zu ihrem Abzug 1991 als Kaserne genutzt.

All that is left today of the picturesque pond and the Olympic Village's Finnish sauna is a green meadow. After the end of the war, the Soviet Army tried to deepen the small pond with heavy machinery. However, the soldiers were surprised to note how fast the water of the pond seeped away. They had accidentally demolished the earthenware slab that architect Werner March had built into the ground of the artificial pond to seal it.

The impressive area served as a window to the world. On the one hand, Olympic participants and journalists were presented an image of a united, peaceful country. On the other hand, modern training facilities and comfortable quarters represented the progressive mindset and capability of the National Socialist state. Reports in the international press about the Olympic Village were mostly positive or even full of admiration. The New York Times, for example, called the accommodations 'magnificent'. The area,

dubbed 'Village of Peace' by the National Socialists, thus fulfilled its purpose.

Before the Games, international protests and calls for a boycott (especially in the US) had jeopardised Berlin's chances to host the Games. The impressive sports facilities, perfect organisation and hitch-free execution, however, gave rise to so much admiration abroad that the IOC decided to let Germany host the 1940 Winter Games as well. This international decision was made after the 'Anschluss' (annexation of Austria), the invasion of German troops in Prague and the November pogroms of 1938. Anti-Semitism and the aggressive foreign policy did not dampen the IOC's enthusiasm a bit. Even then there was a yawning gap between the IOC's rhetoric of political peace and the actual decisions they made.

But the 1936 Summer Games also had an effect on domestic politics. Not only the impressive sports facilities, also the German Olympians represented the

7 — Only the foundations of some of the athletes' quarters in the Olympic Village of Elstal are still discernible.

8 — The gymnasium on the premises is in good condition and hosts exhibitions today.

9 — The swimming stadium during reconstruction work in 2012.

10 — From 1947 until their withdrawal in 1991, the Soviet occupation forces used many parts of the Olympic Village as barracks.

aus dem Osten unter, ab 1947 auch sowjetische Soldaten. Die einzelnen Häuser fanden erneut eine neue Bestimmung. Das Speisehaus der Nationen, das unter der Wehrmacht ein Lazarett war, diente nun als Offiziersschule und wurde später zum Trainingszentrum des sowjetischen Armeesportklubs. Einige olympische Unterkünfte riss die Rote Armee aus Platzmangel ab Mitte der 70er-Jahre ab. An ihrer Stelle entstanden 1983 Plattenbauten. Sie beherbergten das militärische Fachpersonal, das die nuklearen SS-20-Mittelstreckenraketen steuern sollte.

Im Herbst 1991 räumten die sowjetischen Streitkräfte schließlich das Gelände. In den Folgejahren versuchte man einen Investor zu finden, der die Anlage für Wohnzwecke erschließt. Da jedoch niemand bereit war, das beträchtliche finanzielle Risiko einzugehen, wurde das Dorf in den 90er-Jahren zunächst zu einem Anwendungsgebiet für Arbeitsbeschaffungsmaßnahmen. Arbeitslose der Wendejahre hatten Aufräum- und zum Teil auch Restaurationsarbeiten auf dem Gelände zu verrichten. Viele der in Massivbauweise erbauten Häuser verfielen, trotz der fast durchgehenden militärischen Nutzung des Geländes, über die Jahre.

Wer heute über das Gelände spaziert, erwartet vergeblich die erdrückende Strenge einer Kaserne. Vielmehr ist man verwundert, wie idyllisch das Olympische Dorf angelegt wurde. Im Vergleich zum monumentalen Reichssportfeld sind die Gebäude deutlich schlichter gestaltet worden. Die gewundenen Fußwege und einstöckigen Unterkünfte fügen sich harmonisch ins Landschaftsbild ein.

Geht man ein paar Schritte von der teilrestaurierten Schwimmhalle bergab, steht man bald in einem lieblichen Birkenhain. Hier liess Leni Riefenstahl «Fest der Schönheit», ihren zweiten Olympia-Film, beginnen. In der Eingangsszene läuft eine Gruppe Sportler im Morgentau durch ein Wäldchen voll heimischer Tiere. Im nächsten

11 – Dem «Speisehaus der Nationen» wurden immer wieder neue Funktionen zugewiesen.

well-oiled success of the National Socialist regime. In the reasoning of 'völkisch' ideology, they epitomised the superiority of the Aryan race. The sheer number of Olympic medals they won served as proof of that logic. Germany earned 33 gold, 26 silver and 30 bronze medals, relegating the United States to second place by a long way.

Jesse Owens was the sole athlete who was able to mar the athletic success of Nazi Germany at least a little bit. The US-American sprinter won a total of four gold medals in the Berlin Olympic stadium, triumphing over 100 metres, 200 metres, in the sprint relay competition and in long jump. Unexpectedly, the African-American athlete turned into a star and crowd favourite, although he did not succeed in changing the meaning of the Games in any significant way. Possibly his success even reinforced the image of a cosmopolitan Germany propagated by the National Socialists.

Even today, positive memories of the 1936 Summer Olympics still prevail. This could be witnessed recently at a presentation where celebrities in favour of Berlin applying to host the Olympic Games again showed their support. Top chef Tim Raue retold his grandfather's stories of the impressive spirit of the ground-breaking 1936 Summer Games in a completely unreflecting manner, claiming he did not know anything about the exclusion of Jewish athletes, not being a 'political person'. The media reaction was disastrous.

It is not just the memories of the Games, but also the sports facilities of 1936 that have found their own way into the present. The stadiums, halls, grandstands and quarters have been turned into venues of the Football Bundesliga, military barracks, public swimming pools, marching venues, concert stages and museums during the last 80 years. This is an extraordinary development considering that the buildings of a gigantic event,

organised to the last detail and meticulously staged, have been maintained, modernised, and are still used to this day.

Have the Olympic sports facilities become empty stone monuments, completely disconnected from their past? How much of the National Socialist spirit still roams the stadiums today? If Berlin wants to bring the Olympics back to the stage of the biggest propaganda games in the history of sports, these are questions that the city has to face and answer.

Essay von Peter Dittmann

Bild sitzen die muskulösen Athleten gemeinsam nackt in der finnischen Sauna des Olympischen Dorfes und massieren ihre Arme und Beine. Schwitzend schlagen sie sich mit Zweigen auf den Rücken, spurten aus der Holzhütte und springen gekonnt in den dort angelegten Teich. Langsam fährt die Kamera über die nassen, gestählten Männerkörper. Die perfekt anmutenden Athletenkörper strahlen Disziplin, Kraft und Dynamik aus. Riefenstahl zeigt Idealmenschen, Helden, die sich vom Alltäglichen und Durchschnittlichen absetzen.

Vom malerischen Teich und der finnischen Sauna des Olympischen Dorfes ist heute lediglich eine grüne Aue geblieben. Nach Kriegsende hatte die sowjetische Armee versucht, das kleine Gewässer mit schwerem Gerät zu vertiefen. Überrascht mussten die Soldaten jedoch feststellen, dass das Wasser des Teichs schnell versickerte. Sie hatten versehentlich die abdichtenden Tonplatten, die Architekt Werner March im Boden des künstlichen Teiches einbauen liess, zertrümmert.

Die beeindruckende Anlage war ein Schaufenster zur Welt. Zum einen vermittelte sie Olympiateilnehmern wie Journalisten das Bild eines harmonischen, friedlichen Landes. Zum anderen verkörperten moderne Trainingsanlagen und komfortable Unterkünfte die Fortschrittlichkeit und Leistungsfähigkeit des nationalsozialistischen Staates. Die Resonanz auf das Olympische Dorf war in der internationalen Presse dann auch überwiegend positiv bis bewundernd. Die New York Times nannte die Behausungen «magnificent». Die von den Nationalsozialisten «Dorf des Friedens» getaufte Anlage hatte ihren Zweck erfüllt.

Im Vorfeld hatten internationale Proteste und Boykottaufrufe, vor allem in den USA, die Ausrichtung der Spiele in Berlin noch gefährdet. Die beeindruckenden Sportstätten, die perfekte Organisation und reibungslose Durchführung riefen jedoch im Ausland so viel Bewunderung hervor, dass das IOC die Winterspiele für 1940 erneut nach Deutschland vergab. Diese internationale Entscheidung wurde nach dem «Anschluss» Österreichs, dem Einmarsch deutscher Truppen in Prag und dem Novemberprogrom 1938 getroffen. Antisemitismus und aggressive Außenpolitik stellten für das IOC kein Hindernis dar. Schon damals klaffte eine riesige Lücke zwischen sportpolitischer Friedensrhetorik und den tatsächlichen Entscheidungen des IOC.

Auch innenpolitisch verfehlten die Spiele von 1936 ihre Wirkung nicht. Nicht nur die beeindruckenden Sportstätten, auch die deutschen Olympioniken repräsentierten einen funktionierenden, erfolgreichen Nationalsozialismus. In der Logik der völkischen Ideologie verkörperten sie die Überlegenheit der arischen Rasse. Als Nachweis diente der olympische Medaillenspiegel. Mit deutlichem Abstand belegte Deutschland mit 33 Gold-, 26 Silber- und 30 Bronzemedaillen vor den USA den ersten Platz.

Einzig Jesse Owens konnte die sportliche Erfolgsgeschichte des nationalsozialistischen Deutschlands etwas trüben. Im Berliner Olympiastadion gewann der US-amerikanische Sprinter insgesamt vier Goldmedaillen. Er siegte über 100 Meter, 200 Meter, in der Sprintstaffel und im Weitsprung. So wurde ein afroamerikanischer Leichtathlet unerwartet zum Star und Publikumsliebling. Den Spielen eine entscheidend andere Bedeutung zu geben vermochte er freilich nicht. Möglicherweise haben seine Erfolge das von den Nationalsozialisten propagierte Bild eines weltoffenen Deutschlands gar bestärkt.

Bis heute sind positive Erinnerungen an die Olympischen Spiele von 1936 prägend. Das zeigte jüngst Tim Raue bei der Präsentation der prominenten Unterstützer für eine neuerliche Olympiabewerbung Berlins. Unreflektiert erzählte der Spitzenkoch vom beeindruckenden Geist der bahnbrechenden Spiele 1936, die sein Großvater miterlebt habe. Vom Ausschluss jüdischer Sportler wisse er nichts, er sei «kein politischer Mensch». Das Medienecho war verheerend.

Nicht nur die Erinnerungen an die Spiele, auch die Sportstätten von 1936 haben ihren ganz eigenen Weg in die Gegenwart gefunden.

12 – Das Medaillenboot eines deutschen Zweiers von 1936.

13 – Im Wassersportmuseum Berlin-Grünau werden immer noch verschiedene Preziosen der Olympischen Spiele von 1936 aufbewahrt.

11 – The Speisehaus der Nationen (the restaurant of the nations) has been used for many different purposes.

12 – The boat of the German double sculls medalists from the 1936 Olympics.

13 – The Grünauer Water Sports Museum still houses various artefacts of the 1936 Olympic Games.

Aus den Stadien, Hallen, Tribünen und Unterkünften sind in den vergangenen acht Jahrzehnten Spielorte der Fußballbundesliga, Militärkasernen, öffentliche Schwimmbäder, Aufmarschplätze, Konzertbühnen und Museen geworden. Eine aussergewöhnliche Entwicklung, bedenkt man, dass hier die Bauten eines bis ins letzte Detail organisierten und geschickt inszenierten Riesenereignisses erhalten, modernisiert und genutzt werden.

Sind die olympischen Sportstätten etwa nur noch steinerne Hüllen, die sich längst von der Vergangenheit gelöst haben? Wie viel nationalsozialistischer Geist steckt heute noch in den Stadien? Wenn Berlin Olympia zurück an den Schauplatz der größten Propagandaspiele der Sportgeschichte bringen möchte, muss sich die Stadt diesen Fragen stellen.

Peter Dittmann, geboren 1985, ist Politikwissenschaftler sowie freier Journalist mit Schwerpunkt Sportpolitik und lebt in Berlin. Sein Interesse gilt insbesondere Sportgroßereignissen, während der Fußball-EM 2012 war er für drei Monate im Osten der Ukraine, in Donezk. Auf der Suche nach olympischen Geschichten in der eigenen Familie bekam er zunächst den Hinweis, sein Urgroßvater habe an den olympischen Wettkämpfen im 50-Kilometer-Gehen teilgenommen. Nach Recherchen stellte sich jedoch heraus, dass in der Familienerinnerung die sportlichen Leistungen stark verklärt wurden. Der Urgroßvater hatte im Rahmen der Spiele lediglich an Wehrertüchtigungsmärschen mit Gepäck teilgenommen und wurde 24.

Peter Dittmann, born in 1985, is a political scientist and freelance journalist who specialises in sports politics. He lives in Berlin and is especially interested in large sporting events. During the 2012 UEFA European Championship he spent three months in Donetsk in eastern Ukraine. Searching for Olympic stories in his own family he was initially told that his great-grandfather participated in the 50-kilometre race walk during the Summer Olympics. A little research, however, brought to light that family memories of his athletic achievements were hugely embellished. His great-grandfather had merely participated in marches for so-called 'Wehrertüchtigung' (military training for civilians) and came in 24th place.

Olympiastadion Berlin
The Olympic stadium in Berlin

Landhockeyanlage neben dem Olympiastadion
Field hockey facilities next to the Olympic stadium

Glockenturm mit darunter liegender Langemarckhalle
The Langemarckhalle and the towering belfry

Schwimmstadion in direkter Nachbarschaft zum Olympiastadion
The swimming stadium immediately adjacent to the Olympic stadium

Originale Plakatsäule neben einer neuen Imbissbude an der Regattastrecke
An original advertising column next to a new snack bar along the regatta course

Originaltribüne der Regattastrecke in Berlin-Grünau
The original grandstands at the regatta course in Berlin-Grünau

Parcours der Reitanlage
Show-jumping course of the equestrian facilities

Das «Reiterstadion», sanierungsbedürftig, aber wieder in Betrieb
The equestrian stadium is in need of renovations, but operations have been resumed

Abstellraum in der Turnhalle des Olympischen Dorfes
Storage room in the gymnasium of the Olympic Village

Trainingsschwimmhalle im Olympischen Dorf
Indoor training swimming pool in the Olympic Village

Umkleidebereich der Schwimmhalle im Olympischen Dorf
Changing rooms of the indoor swimming pool in the Olympic Village

Russische Plattenbauten auf dem Areal des Olympischen Dorfes
Russian Plattenbauten, pre-fabricated apartment blocks, on the premises of the Olympic Village

«Diskuswerfer» von Karl Albiker neben dem Olympiastadion
The Discus Throwers by Karl Albiker next to the Olympic stadium

SARAJEVO 1984
OLYMPISCHE WINTERSPIELE
———————————————

Das Eis der Geschichte, die Wärme
des Optimismus und das Danach

Essay von Ahmed Burić

SARAJEVO 1984
WINTER OLYMPICS
———————————————

The Ice of the Past, the Warmth
of Optimism and What Came After

Essay by Ahmed Burić

Die Idee zur Veranstaltung der Olympischen Winterspiele in Sarajevo erlebte ihre Geburtsstunde Mitte der 70er-Jahre des 20. Jahrhunderts, und zwar in den Köpfen der bosnisch-herzegowinischen Parteiführung: Die Namen Branko Mikulić, Hamdija Pozderac oder der des damaligen Bürgermeisters von Sarajevo, Dane Maljković, sagen den heutigen Generationen nicht mehr viel, aber die Geschichte des Balkans könnte sie in Erinnerung behalten als Vertreter einer probosnischen Strömung in der zentral gelegenen jugoslawischen Republik, die der unitaristischen Politik Jugoslawiens mit Sitz in Belgrad gegenüberstand. Die Nähe zu Präsident Josip Broz Tito und sein Interesse für dieses Kind des «großen» Jugoslawiens ermöglichte es den bosnischen Machthabern, Tito davon zu überzeugen, dass Sarajevo die Olympischen Spiele braucht. Und davon, dass es sie mit Erfolg organisieren würde, und das in einer Republik, die keinem der drei in ihr lebenden Völkern allein gehörte, sondern allen gleichermassen. Eines der Hauptmerkmale (später auch das Paradoxe) dieser Politik, deren hässlichstes Gesicht sich mit dem Krieg 1992 bis 1995 zeigen würde, war, auf der Vermischung der Völker in Bosnien-Herzegowina zu insistieren: also der Vermischung der Serben, Kroaten und Moslems (heute Bosniaken), welche gemeinsam mit einem kleineren Anteil an Juden und anderen die multiethnische Vielfalt ausmachten. Bosnien-Herzegowina wurde oft als ein Jugoslawien im Kleinen (miss?)verstanden, also war es zu erwarten, dass es wie die gebrechlichste Tochter dieses Landes die besten und die schlechtesten Eigenschaften der «Mutter» in sich trägt.

Die Verletzlichkeit und die Schwäche des Konzeptes «Brüderlichkeit und Einheit», des fundamentalen Credos des Bundes der Kommunisten Jugoslawiens, spiegelte sich am deutlichsten in Bosnien-Herzegowina wider, in welchem die Interessen der benachbarten Republiken Serbien und Kroatien aufeinandertrafen und deren nationale Konzepte,

1 — Ein riesiger Friedhof vor der Olympiahalle «Zetra».

The idea of organising the Olympic Winter Games in Sarajevo was born in the mid-1970s, in the heads of the Bosnian and Herzegovinian leaders of the Communist Party to be precise. The names of Branko Mikulić, Hamdija Pozderac or Dane Maljković, the mayor of Sarajevo at the time, might not sound familiar to today's generations, yet the history of the Balkans might remember them as representatives of the pro-Bosnian segment in the centrally located Yugoslav republic which opposed the Yugoslav unitary politics in Belgrade. Their closeness to President Josip Broz Tito and his interest in this child of the 'great' Yugoslavia enabled the Bosnian leaders to persuade Tito that Sarajevo needed the Olympics. And that they would successfully organise them as well, in a republic which did not belong to any one of the three peoples living in it, but to all of them equally. One of the key concepts of this politics (later a paradox?), which would reveal its ugliest side in the war from 1992 to 1995 was emphasising the heterogeneity of peoples in Bosnia and Herzegovina — Serbs, Croats, and Muslims (now Bosniacs), who, along with a small percentage of Jews and other nationalities, comprised the multi-ethnic diversity of the area. Bosnia and Herzegovina was often (wrongly?!) perceived as a small Yugoslavia; therefore it was expected from this most fragile daughter of the country to have the 'mother's' best and worst qualities.

The vulnerability and weakness of the concept of brotherhood and unity, the main credo of the League of Communists of Yugoslavia, could best be observed in B&H — which was where the interests of the neighbours Croatia and Serbia converged, their national concepts each claiming Bosnia and Herzegovina. It can be said that socialism in B&H was maintained by the firmest grip possible — firmer than that of Belgrade, Zagreb, or Ljubljana. Bosnia and Herzegovina experienced a great wave of industrialisation in the 1960s. Towns grew bigger, and consequently, urban culture developed, giving rise to prominent representatives in literature, music, and sports. Sarajevo and B&H, failing to receive true acknowledgment within their own country, perhaps sought (global) approval that they were doing the right thing. The Winter Olympics seemed to be the perfect opportunity for that. On the one hand, it was high time to catch up with the breeze of capitalism which had already penetrated the Olympic spirit and, on the other hand, one could show the rest of the world that Yugoslav socialism was a stable, almost perfect social system by organising a great spectacle, like the one organised every year on 25 May in celebration of Tito's birthday.

The narcissism of (small) differences

However, things were not at all going smoothly from the very

jedes von seiner Seite, Bosnien-Herzegowina für sich beanspruchten. In diesem Sinne kann man sagen, dass der Sozialismus in Bosnien-Herzegowina von der stärkstmöglichen Hand geleitet wurde – stärker als in Zagreb, Belgrad oder Ljubljana. Ende der 60er-Jahre des 20. Jahrhunderts wurde Bosnien-Herzegowina von einer großen Industrialisierungswelle mitgerissen, die Städte weiteten sich aus und dementsprechend entwickelte sich eine urbane Kultur mit herausragenden Vertretern in Literatur, Musik und Sport. In diesem Sinne haben Sarajevo und Bosnien-Herzegowina vielleicht nach einer (globalen) Bestätigung dafür gesucht, dass sie «das Richtige» tun, weil sie innerhalb des eigenen Staates keine echte Anerkennung bekommen konnten. Die Olympischen Winterspiele schienen das ideale Instrument dafür zu sein: Einerseits musste man den Wind des Kapitalismus, welcher schon ernsthaft den olympischen Geist zu erfassen begann, einfangen, andererseits wollte man mit einer großen Parade, wie man sie jedes Jahr am 25. Mai zum Geburtstag des Präsidenten Tito veranstaltete, dem Rest der Welt zeigen, dass der jugoslawische Sozialismus eine stabile und fast ideale gesellschaftliche Ordnung war.

Der Narzissmus der (kleinen) Unterschiede

Die Sache verlief jedoch von Anfang an nicht glatt. Die damalige jugoslawische Republik Slowenien, heute ein vollwertiges Mitglied der Europäischen Union, schien der ideale Ort für die Olympischen Spiele zu sein. Der Entwicklungsweg sollte in Richtung Wintertourismus führen und dieses Segment wurde im damaligen Jugoslawien exklusiv von Slowenien besetzt. Zeitzeugen zufolge waren die Slowenen von Anfang an enttäuscht, die Olympischen Spiele nicht auf ihrem Territorium austragen zu dürfen. Unstimmigkeiten mit der Staatsspitze durften damals jedoch nicht zu laut geäussert werden.

2/3 – Die Bobbahn auf dem Berg Trebević wurde während der Belagerung Sarajevos zwischen 1992 und 1995 stark beschädigt.

beginning. The former Yugoslav Republic of Slovenia, today a full member of the European Union, seemed to be the perfect place for the Olympics. Winter tourism – a segment in the Socialist Federal Republic of Yugoslavia that until then exclusively belonged to Slovenia – was to be developed. According to accounts from those times, Slovenians were initially disappointed that the Olympics would not be organised in their country, but disagreement with the state leadership could not be voiced too loudly.

The story further goes that the Slovenians were the first to support Sarajevo's proposal to host the Olympics, believing it would be too big a bite for Bosnia and Herzegovina and that the Bosnians would, realising they could not chew it, abandon it in favour of Slovenia. However, in the words of the president of the Socialist Federal Republic of Yugoslavia, Raif Dizdarević, as things developed and the idea was nearing its implementation, the Slovenian leadership tried to dissuade Josip Broz Tito from having the Winter Olympics in Sarajevo. At that point, though, the implementation of the project had already gone too far, and in 1978 Sarajevo was chosen for the Olympics.

A further 'global' side of the story should also be addressed. The Olympic movement had already been deeply affected by the divisions caused by the Cold War. After the boycott of the 1976 Summer Olympics in Montreal by mostly African countries, it was important to ensure that the Games were held in a country that would not be rejected by political powers. The importance of selecting a neutral ground turned out to be justified. The 1980 Summer Olympics in Moscow were not attended by athletes from the USA and its allies. The 'Russians', that is to say the Soviet Union and 14 other socialist countries, responded by not taking part in the 1984 Olympics in Los Angeles. Additionally, voices from Belgrade started to send the message via their

1 – A large cemetery in front of the Zetra Olympic stadium.

2/3 – The bobsleigh track at Trebević mountain was severely damaged during the siege of Sarajevo from 1992 to 1995.

Historisch belegt ist ausserdem, dass die Slowenen als Erste Sarajevo im Bestreben um die Austragung der Winterspiele unterstützten,
in der Überzeugung, dies sei für Bosnien-Herzegowina eine nicht
zu bewältigende Aufgabe und die Bosnier würden, wenn sie dies erst
realisiert hätten, die Angelegenheit den Slowenen überlassen. Als
der Stein jedoch ins Rollen kam und die Idee sich der Realisierung
näherte, versuchte die politische Führung in Slowenien, unterstützt
durch den späteren Präsidenten der Sozialistischen Föderativen
Republik Jugoslawien, Raif Dizdarević, Tito von den Olympischen
Winterspielen in Sarajevo abzuraten. Die Umsetzung des Projekts war
jedoch bereits zu sehr vorangeschritten und Sarajevo bekam 1978
den Zuschlag. Man sollte auch auf die andere, «globale» Seite der
Geschichte zurückblicken: Die damalige olympische Bewegung war
in großem Masse von den Spaltungen erfasst, die der Kalte Krieg mit
sich gebracht hatte. Nachdem 1976 größtenteils afrikanische Länder
die Olympischen Sommerspiele in Montreal boykottiert hatten,
musste darauf geachtet werden, die Spiele nicht dort zu organisieren,
wo sie von politischen Mächten hintertrieben werden konnten. Die
Bedeutung der Wahl eines neutralen Austragungsortes würde sich
als berechtigt erweisen. Schon bei den Olympischen Sommerspielen
in Moskau 1980 blieben die Sportler aus den USA und mit diesen
«alliierte» Nationen fern. Worauf die «Russen», also die Sowjetunion und 14 andere sozialistische Staaten, mit einem Boykott der
Olympischen Spiele in Los Angeles antworteten. Ausserdem begannen
sich auch Gegenstimmen aus Belgrad zu melden, welche über ihre
«liberalen» Presseorgane ausrichten liessen, Bosnien sei mit der
Ausrichtung der Olympischen Spiele überfordert. Nichtsdestoweniger
wurde Sarajevo im Wettstreit mit Sapporo (Japan) und Göteborg
(Schweden) in einer knappen Abstimmung (mit nur zwei Stimmen Unterschied) am 18. Mai 1978 die Veranstaltung zugesprochen.

4 — Die Skisprunganlage auf dem Igman.

'liberal' media that the Olympics would be a bit too much to handle for the Bosnians after all. Nevertheless, competing against Sapporo (Japan) and Gothenborg (Sweden), Sarajevo was chosen to host the Games by a very narrow margin (of only two votes) on 18 May 1978.

Sarajevo, and Yugoslavia, were chosen for the Olympics primarily because of their unique position in the world and a certain willingness to show that this multi-ethnic country, the 'no man's land' between rigid communist Eastern Europe and the firmly capitalist West, could stand on its own two feet.

Today, we know that the Olympics could not have been held in Sarajevo without the help of the West. We will never know the real costs of the 15th Winter Olympics, but from today's perspective, it was economically justified: the organisation cost 142.6 million dollars, yet more than half of the expenditure was covered by the American TV station ABC, which immediately paid 20 million out of the total of 96 million dollars for the broadcasting rights to initiate the construction of infrastructure.

It is difficult to believe that anything would have been possible without this initial investment. However, economic justification was not the biggest motive for the Sarajevo Olympics.

Yugoslavia was at that time shaken by its biggest economic crisis, causing a lack of fuel as well as other basic commodities such as cooking oil, flour, coffee… External debt had increased from 6.5 billion dollars in 1975 to 20.5 billion in 1983. The concept of socialist self-governance was deeply shaken, while Josip Broz Tito's death in 1980 made the discrepancies more obvious and further aggravated the existing problems. The average salary in 1985 was inflated to the average of 1967. When the crisis was publicly recognised in 1981, the construction of Olympic facilities was already well under way. The media mostly reported success stories, avoiding to cover the increasing number of strikes. Yet, it seemed to not have affected the Olympic project as 75 per cent out of 250,000 tickets were sold outside of Yugoslavia. The legacy of the Olympics also included 2,850 new flats and 9,500 new jobs.

President Tito's
last birthday

If the theorists of totalitarianism are correct in saying that the human body is the basic shape that mirrors the rigidity of a political system, it can be said that the opening ceremony of the Sarajevo Olympics was one of the most beautiful faces of totalitarianism one could imagine. Only today does the writer of these lines understand the words uttered by Nobel Prize winner Herta Müller, a German with Romanian roots, a few years ago, 'You know, in contrast to Romanian socialism, yours was — sexy. All those girls with full breasts at parades.' In reality, the breasts of the beautiful girls from Sarajevo,

Sarajevo und Jugoslawien erhielten den Zuschlag für die Organisation der Winterspiele vor allem aufgrund ihrer spezifischen Lage auf der Weltkarte, aber auch aus einer Art Interesse heraus, ob dieses multinationale Land, dieser «Pufferstaat» zwischen dem rigiden, kommunistischen Osteuropa und dem «freien», kapitalistischen Westen, auf eigenen Beinen stehen könne.

Heute wissen wir, dass diese Olympischen Spiele ohne die Hilfe des Westens nicht zustande gekommen wären. Den wirklichen Preis für die 14. Olympischen Winterspiele werden wir nie erfahren, aber aus heutiger Perspektive kann man sagen, dass sie ökonomisch nicht ungerechtfertigt waren: Die Organisation kostete zwar 142,6 Millionen Dollar, mehr als die Hälfte dieser Ausgaben wurde jedoch durch den amerikanischen Fernsehsender ABC gedeckt, welcher von den 96 Millionen, die die Fernsehübertragungsrechte kosteten, 20 Millionen sofort überwies und somit den Start des Baus der Anlagen ermöglichte.

Es ist schwer zu glauben, dass Bosnien ohne diese Anfangsinvestition die Vorbereitungen auch nur beginnen hätte können. Nichtsdestoweniger war die ökonomische Sinnhaftigkeit nicht das stärkste Motiv der Olympischen Spiele in Sarajevo. Jugoslawien wurde damals von einer schweren Wirtschaftskrise geschüttelt, die sich in einem Mangel an Benzin, aber auch an Grundnahrungsmitteln spiegelte: Speiseöl, Mehl, Kaffee … Die Auslandsverschuldung stieg von 6,5 Milliarden Dollar im Jahr 1975 auf 20,5 Milliarden im Jahr 1983 an. Das Konzept der sozialistischen Selbstverwaltung war ernsthaft erschüttert und mit dem Tod von Tito 1980 wurden die Gegensätze noch offensichtlicher und die Probleme immer größer. Die Inflation brachte das Durchschnittsgehalt im Jahr 1985 auf das Niveau von 1967. Als 1981 die Krise öffentlich eingestanden wurde, war die Errichtung der olympischen Objekte in vollem Gange, die Medien berichteten hauptsächlich über die Erfolge und nicht darüber, dass auch die

5 — Das Skisprung-Jurorenhaus ist nach starkem Zerfall aus Sicherheitsgründen gesperrt worden.

who carried the participant countries' flags, could not be seen, as they were wearing fashionable ski suits, but beauty could indeed be witnessed everywhere. Ms Müller was in fact referring to the Yugoslav custom of celebrating Marshal Tito's birthday. The celebration was called 'slet', which can roughly be translated as performance or spectacle, and it included the performance of hundreds of young, beautiful people who exhibited playfulness as well as readiness to defend socialism. It was customary to offer birthday greetings on every 25 May at the stadium of the Yugoslav People's Army, with pompous choreography and the participation of the army. The highlight of the event was the presentation of the baton which had travelled through all the republics and provinces in the hands of youth.

The youth appointed to give the baton to Tito in his VIP lounge would run up a few dozen stairs and still out of breath utter: 'Our dear Comrade Tito, we,

the youth and pioneers, wish you a happy birthday and hope for you to guide Yugoslavia along the paths of brotherhood and unity for many years to come.' This is how the youth showed loyalty to their president; therefore it could be said that the opening ceremony of the Winter Olympics in Sarajevo was the last celebration of Tito's birthday, four years after his death.

The Olympic torch (baton) was lit by ice skater Sanda Dubravčić; and all elements of a spectacle showing that Yugoslavia was a stable country and the Olympic spirit at its peak were fulfilled. One of the best anecdotes from these times says that 5,000 Yugoslav soldiers from barracks in Sarajevo were on stand-by to operate the snow machines necessary for skiing competitions day and night, should the Olympics begin without snow. However, as the mountains around the B&H capital turned abundantly white, those same soldiers had to pace and jump along the ski slopes to flatten

4 — The Igman Olympic Jumps.

5 — The gravely deteriorated judges tower has been closed for security reasons.

Anzahl an Streiks zunahm. Dies schien das Projekt Olympische Spiele jedoch nicht weiter zu stören, da von den 250 000 Eintrittskarten 75 Prozent ausserhalb Jugoslawiens verkauft wurden, nach den Spielen 2850 neue Wohnungen bezogen werden konnten und zusätzliche 9500 Arbeitsplätze geschaffen wurden.

Der letzte Geburtstag des Präsidenten Tito

Wenn die Theoretiker des Totalitarismus recht haben mit ihrer Behauptung, dass der menschliche Körper die Grundform ist, in welcher sich die Rigidität eines politischen Systems widerspiegelt, dann kann man sagen, dass die Eröffnung der Winterspiele in Sarajevo eines der schönsten Gesichter des Totalitarismus war, das man sich vorstellen kann. Erst heute versteht der Autor dieses Essays die Worte, die die Nobelpreisträgerin Herta Müller vor ein paar Jahren sprach:

«Wissen Sie, im Unterschied zu unserem rumänischen Sozialismus war der Ihre – *sexy*. All diese Mädchen, deren Brüste auf diesen Paraden zur Geltung kamen.» Um bei der Wahrheit zu bleiben: Die Brüste wunderschöner Mädchen aus Sarajevo, die bei der Eröffnung der Spiele die Transparente der Wettbewerbsländer trugen, konnte man zwar nicht sehen, da sie moderne Skianzüge trugen, aber Schönheit konnte man überall antreffen. Freilich hatte Frau Müller die jugoslawischen Feiern zu Ehren des Geburtstags Marschall Titos im Sinn. Bei diesen Manifestationen, die unter dem Namen «slet» liefen, wirkten Hunderte von jungen und schönen Menschen mit, die Verspieltheit zeigten, aber auch die Bereitschaft, den Sozialismus zu verteidigen. Sitte war es nämlich, an jedem 25. Mai im JNA-Stadion in Belgrad Marschall Tito mit einer pompösen Choreografie und unter Mitwirkung der Armee zum Geburtstag zu gratulieren. Der Höhepunkt dieses Ereignisses war die Übergabe einer Stafette, welche zuvor in den

6 – Das Olympische Dorf «Mojmilo» wurde auch mit Hilfe und Geld der Stadt Barcelona wieder aufgebaut.

about one metre of snow that had fallen overnight. It seemed that heaven was siding with those who did not believe in it – the communist society was deeply atheist, of course – and that a winter tale was unfolding. The tale which would end with the embrace of (proto)capitalism and (real) socialism, the reconciliation of West and East in the city that had until then been known as the starting point of World War I.

Danse macabre:
sobering up after the feast

The country whose workers were 'on ice' and whose elite lived a bourgeois lifestyle organised what was said to be 'the best Olympic Games in history'. Certainly, all Games thereafter were also 'the best', but Sarajevo was for a long time acknowledged and thanked for accomplishing such a great job. The graphic design of Bosnian and Herzegovinian artists was in no way lacking behind compared to that of designs from

Moscow or Lake Placid; the universal spirit of the Olympics seemed as if it would live on forever in this key city in the mountains. The Olympics in Sarajevo were to a certain extent a monument to socialist Yugoslavia and an acknowledgment that it successfully struck a balance between the extremes. What was overlooked was the fact that this region had never grown out of the concept of nationalist states and that the celebration of the Olympics was actually a dance on a graveyard.

And this is exactly what the surroundings of the Olympic facilities showed in 1992 when the city was under siege and the dead could not be buried on the slopes of the hills. Instead, the land around the Zetra and Koševo stadiums had to be used as cemeteries for those killed during the siege. It is impossible to count all the reasons for the disintegration of Yugoslavia, but two of them are very obvious: this country with great potential for nationalism, in which it was the army who had

the last word, was unable to bear the internal pressure and simply exploded. This very explosion was initiated by the army itself as, unable to undergo a transformation and become the army of the newly formed states on Yugoslav ground, it put itself under the command of Serb nationalists.

That was a spin that condemned the country to disaster: only eight years after the Olympics, the Olympic flame was replaced by the fire of artillery. Before that, Yugoslavia collapsed, first in economic terms and then spiritually. The chance to join the European Union was wasted, and Serbian President Milošević destroyed the country under the pretence of protecting the very same. The troubles in the country were additionally aggravated by the confusion and inefficiency of the international community, which in the beginning trusted Mislošević's nationalists. It is perhaps a paradox that the socialism which had been claimed to be the most liberal – 'better'

Händen von Jugendlichen durch alle Republiken und Provinzen gereist war. Die auserwählten Jugendlichen, die Tito in der festlichen Loge die Stafette überreichen durften, liefen mehrere Dutzend Treppen hoch und sprachen, meistens ausser Atem, folgende Worte: «Lieber Kamerad Tito, wir Jugendlichen und Pioniere wünschen dir alles Gute zum Geburtstag und dass du Jugoslawien noch lange auf dem Weg entlang der Brüderlichkeit und Einheit führst.» Jugendliche demonstrierten auf diese Art und Weise dem Präsidenten ihre Ergebenheit, daher könnte man sagen, dass die Eröffnung der Olympischen Winterspiele in Sarajevo die letzte Geburtstagsfeier Titos war, vier Jahre nach seinem Tod.

Das olympische Feuer (die Stafette) zündete die Eisläuferin Sanda Dubravčić an, und alle Beteiligten des Spektakels, welches zeigen sollte, dass Jugoslawien ein stabiles Land war und der olympische Geist seine besten Zeiten durchlebte, waren zufriedengestellt. Eine der besten Anekdoten aus dieser Zeit erzählt von 5000 Soldaten der Jugoslawischen Volksarmee aus der Kaserne in Sarajevo, die in Bereitschaft waren – falls die Spiele ohne Schnee beginnen sollten –, Tag und Nacht an den (Schnee-)Kanonen an der Herstellung des für den Skisport unverzichtbaren Schnees zu arbeiten. Als die Berge in der Umgebung der Hauptstadt Bosnien-Herzegowinas jedoch reichlich in Weiß erstrahlten, mussten genau diese Soldaten auf den Pisten auf und ab stapfen, um den Meter Neuschnee, der über Nacht gefallen war, auszutreten. Es schien, als wäre sogar der Himmel auf der Seite derer, die nicht an ihn glaubten – die kommunistische Gesellschaft war ja eine zutiefst atheistische –, und dass ein Wintermärchen wahr würde. Ein Märchen, welches in einer Umarmung zwischen dem (Proto-)Kapitalismus und dem (Real-)Sozialismus endete, der Versöhnung zwischen Ost und West, und das in einer Stadt, die bis dahin dafür bekannt gewesen war, dass in ihr der 1. Weltkrieg seinen Ausgangspunkt hatte.

7 – Das Olympische Dorf, im Westen Sarajevos, ist heute wieder ein lebendiger Ort.

than that in the USSR, Albania, Bulgaria, Czechoslovakia – suffered the bloodiest end of all. Under such circumstances, universal ideas had no chance of survival.

The degradation and destruction of Olympic facilities during the attacks on Bosnia and Herzegovina seemed like the last act of this *danse macabre,* in the century that can be epitomised by the metaphor of the concentration camp. Sarajevo was an Olympic concentration camp. There, it was possible that on European soil, in the city symbolising Olympic triumph, Serbian soldiers controlled the city and all movement in it with gunfire, like in some war video game. Ice skating was replaced by dragging water containers on ice and instead of biathlon, other sports disciplines developed, such as running from sniper fire or hiding from shell fire or extinguishing fire. War times demanded different 'skills' – Sarajevo, and Bosnia and Herzegovina as a whole, was consumed by the

epidemic of nationalism, which left no room for the aesthetics of the Olympics or high achievement. Nationalism in itself is a closed concept and rarely, almost never, does it produce a world hero or an Olympic champion. Just as the world champion in amateur and professional boxing Mate Parlov, a Yugoslav hero of the 1970s and 1980s, nicely explained once when asked if he was a nationalist: 'I cannot be a nationalist, I was the world champion.'

The concept of neglect: once upon a time, there were Olympic Games

The end of the war in Bosnia and Herzegovina and the victory of nationalist parties shed light on the outdatedness and backwardness of the Southern Slavic nationalist societies. One can say that we are today as far away from the Olympics as we are from more or less successful societies of Western Europe. Therefore, the idea of organising the Olympics

6 – The Mojmilo Olympic Village was built with assistance and funds from the city of Barcelona.

7 – The Olympic Village, in the west of Sarajevo, has developed into a lively place again.

Danse macabre: die Ernüchterung nach der Feier

Das Land, dessen Arbeiter nicht in Wohlstand lebten, dessen Elite jedoch das Leben der Bourgeoisie führte, hatte, so erzählte man sich damals, die «besten Olympischen Spiele der Geschichte» organisiert. Natürlich waren alle darauffolgenden jeweils die «besten», aber Sarajevo erhielt noch lange nach den Spielen Bestätigung und Danksagungen dafür, dass es damals Großes geleistet hatte. Das graphische Design der Künstler Bosnien-Herzegowinas stand jenen in Moskau oder Lake Placid in nichts nach, und es schien, als ob diese historisch wichtige Bergstadt den universalistischen olympischen Geist für immer beheimaten würde. Die Olympischen Spiele in Sarajevo waren ein einzigartiges Denkmal für das sozialistische Jugoslawien und eine Anerkennung dafür, dass es erfolgreich zwischen den Extremen balancieren konnte. Was man nicht bedacht hatte, war, dass dieser Raum niemals sein Konzept der Nationalstaaten ausgelebt hatte und dass das Zelebrieren der Olympischen Spiele in Wahrheit ein Fest auf einem Friedhof war.

Die Umgebung der olympischen Objekte wird 1992 genau das demonstrieren, als die Stadt belagert wird und man die Toten nicht auf Hügeln begraben kann, sondern die Umgebung der Olympiahalle Zetra und des Stadions Koševo zu Friedhöfen für diejenigen, die während der Belagerung fallen, umfunktioniert werden muss. Es ist unmöglich, sämtliche Gründe für den Zerfall Jugoslawiens in diesem Text anzuführen, aber die zwei Hauptgründe sind unbestritten: Ein Land mit so vielen potenziellen Nationalismen, in welchem im Grunde das Heer das Sagen hatte, konnte einem solchen inneren Druck nicht standhalten und musste schlicht und einfach explodieren. Die Initialzündung für diese Explosion erfolgte durch genau jene Armee, die sich unter das Kommando des serbischen Nationalismus stellte, da sie unfähig war,

8 — Der Turm im Olympiapark «Zetra» ist umgeben von Gräbern. Sie stammen aus der Belagerungszeit in den 1990er-Jahren, als man nicht mehr wusste, wohin mit den Toten.

in Sarajevo in 2014 to celebrate the 30th anniversary was just a sentimental outcry of those who still remember that it really used to be better. The Yugoslav society, for the most part of its existence, was not democratic but to a great extent functional. Apart from being democratic just on the surface, today's society is not functional. This is illustrated by its attitude towards the Olympic facilities. Today, Zetra, once a project of international reputation, is far from properly maintained and run with great difficulties. There is a half-torn-up sign above the western entrance, the delivery entrance, which says 'Welcome to the Zetra Olympic hall'. While it is still technically possible to go skating or play hockey in Zetra, no competition could now be organised on the bobsleigh tracks or ski jumping hills. The company ZOI 84, which is responsible for the Olympic facilities, is today just a broken giant on its knees. The employees have for years not been

paid their salaries; directors, unable to settle financial debts, resign one after another, only prolonging the agony of the formerly strong Olympic company. Due to the enormous debts, it is no longer possible to try to save some Olympic facilities by finding investors for them: the ZOI company's debt for electric utilities alone amounts to an incredible 206,030.59 convertible marka. Such a collapse of infrastructure is a result of handling privately and publicly owned property recklessly, which was one of the reasons why socialism failed.

The memory of the Olympics is a collective one. It belongs to all of us and it can be said that what was once called social ownership has turned into public property. As today nobody cares about public goods, it has not been made possible for private investors to buy public property. So the Olympic snow flake, the symbol of the 1984 Olympics, melted. The mascot Vučko, a cute wolf on skis with a scarf, the work of

Slovenian painter Jože Trobec, is now just a symbol of the past, which smiles at us from cheap wooden souvenirs.

Today's Sarajevo sadly cannot be called an Olympic city anymore. It is a city that once hosted the Olympic Games; but also the city that will have to wait for that state of mind to be perhaps formed again. Nowhere else do the forces of progress and destruction interchange as much as in Southeast Europe. 39 years passed between the end of World War II and the Sarajevo Olympics. It has been 20 years since the last war and Sarajevo still very much feels the consequences of that conflict. All we have left now is the hope that the forces of progress will not take as long as they did in the past to reunite for noble ideas. For this to happen, our attitude towards the past as well as the present has to change.

For our own good and for the survival of the Olympic movement.

die Transformation in eine Armee der neuen (auf dem Gebiet des ehemaligen Jugoslawiens entstandenen) Staaten zu vollziehen.

Das war der Auslöser, der das Land in den Ruin führte: Nur acht Jahre nach den Olympischen Spielen wird sich die olympische Fackel in einen Artilleriesturm verwandeln. Jugoslawien kollabiert, zuerst im ökonomischen, dann auch im geistigen Sinne. Die Chance auf einen Eintritt in die Gemeinschaft der Europäer wird vertan, und der serbische Präsident wird das Land, unter dem Vorwand, er wolle es beschützen, zerstören. Die Angelegenheit wurde zusätzlich durch die Verwirrung und Ineffizienz der Internationalen Organisationen erschwert, welche zunächst Miloševićs Nationalisten Glauben schenkten. Vielleicht ist es paradox, aber der Sozialismus, von dem man behauptete, er wäre der liberalste gewesen – «besser» als der in der UdSSR, Albanien, Bulgarien, der Tschechoslowakei –, löste sich in Blut auf. In solch einer Situation hatten die universalistischen Ideen die geringsten Überlebenschancen.

Die Verwüstung der olympischen Anlagen während der Aggression gegen Bosnien-Herzegowina wirkte wie der letzte Akt eines *Danse macabre,* in einem Jahrhundert, in dem die stärkste Metapher das Konzentrationslager ist. Sarajevo war ein olympisches Konzentrationslager, in dem es den serbischen Soldaten möglich war, auf europäischem Boden in einer Olympiastadt von den umliegenden Bergen aus wie in einem Videospiel die Stadt und das Leben in ihr mit Waffengewalt zu kontrollieren. Der Eiskunstlaufwettbewerb wurde durch das Schleppen der Wasserkanister auf Eis ersetzt, und an die Stelle des Langlaufs traten andere (Sport-)Disziplinen wie das Fliehen vor Scharfschützen, das Versteckspiel mit Granaten oder das Feuerlöschen. Die Kriegszeiten lehrten andere Disziplinen und Sarajevo sowie Bosnien-Herzegowina wurden von einer Epidemie des Nationalismus zerfressen, einer, in der es keinen Platz für olympische Ästhetik gab, und auch kein Potenzial für große Errungenschaften. Der Nationalismus an sich ist ein geschlossenes Konzept, und er produziert selten, so gut wie nie, einen internationalen Helden oder Olympiasieger. Genauso wie einmal der Weltmeister im Amateur- und Profiboxen, der Held der jugoslawischen 70er- und 80er-Jahre des vergangenen Jahrhunderts, Mate Parlov, in einem Interview die Frage, ob er Nationalist sei, so schön beantwortete: «Ich kann kein Nationalist sein, ich war Weltmeister.»

Das «Konzept» der Verwahrlosung: Es waren einmal die Olympischen Spiele

Mit dem Ende des Bosnienkriegs und dem Sieg der nationalistischen Konzepte kam die Rückständigkeit der nationalistischen, südslawischen Gesellschaften zum Vorschein. Heute könnte man sagen, dass wir von den Olympischen Spielen so weit entfernt sind wie unser Gesellschaftssystem von relativ erfolgreichen Gesellschaften Westeuropas. Daher zeugt die Idee von Olympischen Spielen in Sarajevo 2014 zum 30-jährigen Jubiläum von einem verklärenden Wahn derjenigen, die sich daran erinnern, dass es einmal wirklich besser war. Die jugoslawische Gesellschaft war in den seltensten Momenten ihres Bestehens demokratisch, aber in den allermeisten funktional. Die heutigen Systeme sind, abgesehen davon, dass sie nur oberflächlich demokratisch sind, nicht funktional, was am deutlichsten im Umgang mit «olympischer Architektur» sichtbar wird. Die Zetra-Halle, einst ein Projekt von internationalem Ruf, kämpft heute mit großen Schwierigkeiten und ist völlig unrentabel. Über dem westlichen, für Frachtgut vorgesehenen Eingang hängt ein halb zerrissenes Schild: «Willkommen in der Olympiahalle Zetra». Und während man die Zetra-Halle, zumindest vom technischen Standpunkt aus, immer noch betreten kann, um eiszulaufen oder um Hockey zu spielen, sind die Bobbahnen und Skisprungschanzen zurzeit nicht wettbewerbstauglich. Das Unternehmen ZOI 84, unter dessen Verwaltung auch die olympischen Objekte stehen, ist heute ein ehemaliger Gigant auf Knien. Die Arbeiter

9 – Das Eisstadion «Zetra» wurde während eines Bombardements 1992 fast komplett zerstört und diente während des Kriegs auch als Leichenhalle oder Medizinallager.

10 – Nach dem Krieg wurde das Gebäude wieder aufgebaut. Es wird heute als Multifunktionshalle genutzt.

8 – Graves surround the Zetra Olympic Park tower. They were built during the siege in the 1990s, when the city ran out of burial sites.

9 – The Zetra ice stadium was almost completely destroyed by an air raid in 1992 and also served as a morgue and a storage site for medicine during the war.

10 – The building was re-erected after the war. It is used as a multi-purpose hall today.

werden seit Jahren nicht entlohnt, Direktoren, die die Schulden nicht sanieren konnten, mussten einer nach dem anderen erfolglos aufgeben und nur die Agonie, in der sich die einst große olympische Firma befand, hat sich vertieft. Jetzt ist es schon zu spät dafür, mithilfe partieller Investitionen den Versuch zu machen, einzelne olympische Objekte zu retten, denn die Schulden sind horrend: Allein die unbezahlten Stromrechnungen der Firma ZOI belaufen sich auf unglaubliche 206 030,59 Konvertible Mark. Ein derartiger Zerfall der Infrastruktur ist ein Hinweis auf einen zu lockeren Umgang mit privatem und öffentlichem Eigentum, was einer der Gründe ist, weshalb der Sozialismus zusammengebrochen ist. Die Erinnerungen an die Olympischen Spiele sind kollektiv. Sie gehören uns allen, und man kann mit Recht behaupten, dass dieses damalige öffentliche Eigentum heute zu einem Allgemeingut geworden ist. Da sich heute niemand um öffentliches Eigentum schert, wurde privaten Investoren kein Erwerb ermöglicht. So ist die Schneeflocke, das Wahrzeichen der Olympischen Winterspiele 1984, geschmolzen. Das Maskottchen Vučko, ein sympathischer Wolf mit Schal auf Skiern, der vom slowenischen Maler Jože Trobec entworfen worden war, ist heute nur ein Symbol der Vergänglichkeit, welches uns von billigen Holzsouvenirs aus anlächelt.

Heute kann man von Sarajevo leider nicht behaupten, es sei eine olympische Stadt. Es ist vielmehr eine Stadt, in der einmal die Olympischen Spiele abgehalten wurden. Und es ist eine Stadt, die noch lange darauf warten wird, dass sich dieses Bewusstsein ändert. Die Kräfte des Fortschritts und der Zerstörung wechseln sich wohl nirgends so stark ab wie in Südosteuropa. Seit dem Ende des 2. Weltkriegs bis zu den Olympischen Spielen in Sarajevo sind 39 Jahre vergangen. Seit dem letzten Krieg bis heute sind es 20, und Sarajevo leidet noch immer an den Folgen dieses schweren bewaffneten Konflikts. Es bleibt nur zu hoffen, dass fortschrittliche Kräfte nicht so lange warten werden wie in der Vergangenheit, um edlere Ideen zu entfalten. Aber damit das geschieht, muss man den Bezug sowohl zur Vergangenheit als auch zur Gegenwart ändern.

Zu unser aller Wohl und für den Fortbestand der olympischen Bewegung.

Ahmed Burić, geboren 1967 in Sarajevo, studierte Journalismus an der Fakultät für Politikwissenschaften. Er ist Schriftsteller, Dichter, Übersetzer, Journalist und Herausgeber. Er veröffentlichte mehrere Tausend Texte für liberale Medien in ganz Osteuropa. Zurzeit ist er Kolumnist für Radio Sarajevo, eines der meistgelesenen Webportale Südosteuropas. Seine Stimme gilt als unverkennbar. Er lebt in Sarajevo.

Ahmed Burić, born in Sarajevo in 1967, studied journalism at the Institute of Political Science. He is an author, poet, translator, journalist and publisher. He has published several thousand texts for liberal media across Eastern Europe. He currently works as a columnist for Radio Sarajevo, one of the most widely visited web portals in Southeast Europe. He is known for his distinctive voice. He lives in Sarajevo.

Olympia-Eishalle «Skenderija» im Zentrum von Sarajevo
The Skenderija Olympic ice stadium in the centre of Sarajevo

Olympiapark «Zetra»
The Zetra Olympic Park

Trainingsplätze neben dem Stadion «Zetra»
Training courts next to the Zetra stadium

Vom Berg Trebević aus wurde Sarajevo beschossen
Sarajevo was bombarded from Trebević mountain

Von der Natur eingenommen: Bobbahn am Berg Trebević
Conquered by nature: the bobsleigh track on Trebević mountain

Verlassenes Gebäude auf dem Trebević
Deserted building on Trebević mountain

Betonröhre im bosnischen Wald
Concrete bobsleigh track in the Bosnian forest

Observatorium unweit der Bobbahn
Observatory close to the bobsleigh track

Blick von der großen Sprungschanze zum Stadion
View of the stadium from the top of the large ski jump

Bosnischer Tourist beim Siegerpodium der Skisprunganlage
A Bosnian tourist at the winners' rostrum of the ski-jump venue

01

Skisprunganlage auf dem Igman
The Igman Olympic Jumps

Jurorenhaus der Skisprunganlage
The judges tower at the ski-jump venue

Hotel Igman an der im Krieg umkämpften Hauptstraße nach Sarajevo
Hotel Igman on the main road to Sarajevo, which was the location of many fights during the war

Olympisches Dorf «Mojmilo» in Sarajevo
The Mojmilo Olympic Village in Sarajevo

Muhamed Sabic vor dem Club der Pensionäre im Olympischen Dorf
Muhamed Sabic in front of the pensioners' club in the Olympic Village

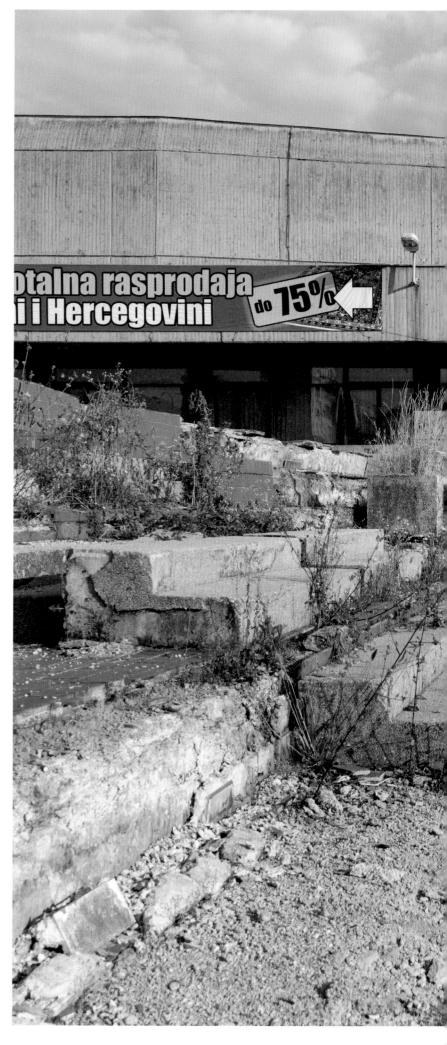

Eishockeyhalle «Skenderija» im Zentrum Sarajevos
The Skenderija Olympic ice stadium in the centre of Sarajevo

Blick aus dem Eisstadion «Zetra»
View from the Zetra ice stadium

TURIN 2006
OLYMPISCHE WINTERSPIELE
────────────────────

Acht Jahre danach

Essay von Francesco Pastorelli

TURIN 2006
WINTER OLYMPICS
────────────────────

Eight Years Later

Essay by Francesco Pastorelli

29. September 2014: Wir befinden uns im Ratssaal der Gemeinde Oulx im Susatal, acht Jahre nach den Olympischen Winterspielen in Turin. Das Tal im Piemont hatte Teile des Sportanlasses ausgetragen. «Für uns waren die Olympischen Spiele eine Katastrophe! Von 50 Hektar unseres Unternehmens wurden 20 von der Biathlonanlage in Anspruch genommen, für deren Umsetzung das Gelände verändert wurde. Man säte Futterpflanzen, die rein gar nichts mit unserer Region zu tun haben.» Daniele Barmond, Landwirt und Geschäftsführer eines Agriturismo in San Sicario, gibt seinem Unmut im Rahmen des *Laboratorio alpino per lo sviluppo* von CIPRA Italia (italienische Sektion der Internationalen Alpenschutzkommission) Ausdruck, zu welchem er zur Präsentation seiner Erfahrungen als junger Berglandwirt eingeladen worden war. Er fährt fort: «Die Weiden, die an die Bobbahn angrenzen, können wir nur mit großer Mühe mähen. Im Jahr nach den Spielen verursachte die Arbeit Schäden von über 3000 Euro an den landwirtschaftlichen Apparaten – infolge unterschiedlicher Abfallmaterialien wie Gitter, Alteisen oder Betonbruchstücken, die auf den Rasenflächen zurückgelassen worden sind.»

28. September 2014: Elf Rumänen wurden unter der Anklage von Raub und Hehlerei festgenommen. Sie waren beim Diebstahl von Kupfer auf dem Terrain der olympischen Bobbahn von Cesana Pariol überrascht worden. Es ist nicht schwierig, die Einzäunung zu überwinden, welche die verbleibende Bobanlage umzäunt – schon gar nicht für professionelle Diebe.

2. August 2014: Turin, Wohnhaus des ehemaligen Olympischen Dorfes, Quartier Lingotto. Bei einer der unzähligen Schlägereien zwischen Immigranten wurden zwei Personen erstochen. Die Häuser, welche die Athleten während der Turniere bewohnten, waren damals als Gebäudekomplexe nach modernsten, innovativen Energieeffizienzkriterien errichtet worden. Heute befinden sie sich in einem deso-

1 – Der Biathlonschießstand im tief verschneiten San Sicario.

29 September 2014: eight years after the Winter Olympics in Turin, we are in the town council meeting room of the municipality of Oulx in Val di Susa, one of the valleys of Piedmont that hosted the Games. 'The Olympics were a disaster for us! The biathlon course has had an impact on 20 of the 50 hectares of our farm; to construct the course, it was necessary to modify the land profile and sow forage species totally foreign to the area.' Daniele Barmond, farmer and manager of a holiday farm in San Sicario, delivers this statement in the course of the Alpine Development Workshop organised by CIPRA Italia, the Italian chapter of the International Commission for the Protection of the Alps, where he was asked to describe his experiences as a young mountain farmer. He goes on to say: 'We find it very difficult to cut the grass in the meadows next to the bobsleigh track. The year after the Games, various materials, grilles as well as steel and concrete chunks, which were left behind throughout the meadows, caused 3,000 euros worth of damage to our farm machinery.'

28 September 2014: eleven Romanians are arrested and charged with theft and receiving stolen goods after being caught stealing copper at the Cesana Pariol bobsleigh track. It is not difficult to slip through the fence that encloses what is left of the bobsleigh track, especially for professional thieves.

2 August 2014: Turin, the buildings of the former Olympic Village in the Lingotto area. Two people are stabbed during the umpteenth brawl among immigrants. The blocks of flats that housed the athletes during the Games, heralded at the time as a cutting-edge residential complex fulfilling modern energy-efficiency criteria, are beyond repair. In 2013, immigrants and refugees from North Africa moved in. The plaster of the façades is falling off, graffiti and decay dominate, and tension permeates this lower-income neighbourhood. This is far from a renewal of the area, but at least the Olympic Village shelters a disadvantaged part of the population.

6 December 2014: a Serie A football match between Turin and Palermo is played at the Olympic stadium. About 14,000 shivering spectators are attending. The playing field is far removed from the stands. There is not even a running track to separate the spectators from the field, as was the case in the old Comunale stadium, on top of which this stadium was built. This stadium was designed and built exclusively to host the Games' opening ceremony… at a cost of over 30 million euros. Now it is being adapted for football games, but the fans do not like it at all. In the meantime, Turin's other stadium, the Delle Alpi, which was built for the 1990 World Cup, was demolished (after less than 15 years of use) and the land and the related building rights were donated to Juventus, the football team of the company FIAT, which used it to build its

laten Zustand und werden seit 2013 von Flüchtlingen und Vertriebenen aus Nordafrika bewohnt. Der Fassadenverputz zerfällt, Schriften auf den Mauern und allgemeiner Verfall dominieren. Im ehemals berühmten Quartier herrscht eine angespannte Atmosphäre. Es wäre wohl anmaßend, die Gesamtsanierung des Quartiers ins Auge zu fassen, aber zumindest haben einige arme Personen ein sicheres Obdach erhalten.

6. Dezember 2014: Im Olympiastadion wird das Fußballspiel der Meisterschaft der Serie A zwischen Turin und Palermo ausgetragen. Etwa 14 000 Zuschauer fiebern bei kaltem Wetter mit. Die Distanz zwischen Spielfeld und Zuschauertribüne ist überaus groß. Dabei gibt es nicht einmal eine Athletenbahn, die die Rasenfläche von den Tribünen trennen würde, wie zu Zeiten des alten Comunale, auf dessen Fundament das Olympiastadion steht. Das neue Stadion wurde exklusiv als Austragungsort der Eröffnungszeremonie der Spiele entworfen. Mehr als 30 Millionen Euro betrugen die Kosten. Heute wird es für Fußballspiele genutzt. Den Fans gefällt es ganz und gar nicht. In der Zwischenzeit wurde das andere Turiner Stadion namens Delle Alpi, zum Anlass der Fußballweltmeisterschaft 1990 errichtet, zurückgebaut, nach nicht einmal 15 Jahren Nutzung. Das Gelände mit Baunutzung schenkte man Juventus, dem Fußballverein der Firma Fiat, die sich dort ein eigenes Privatstadion inklusive Einkaufszentrum aufstellte.

So erging es Italien – und Turin – zu Anfang des dritten Millenniums.

Die Olympischen Spiele von Turin, ein organisatorischer und prestigeträchtiger Erfolg mit vielen Einschränkungen

Die 15-tägigen Winterspiele verliefen wie geplant: Die nahezu perfekte Organisation war in aller Munde. Das positive Image von Turin

2 – Das «Stadio Olimpico»: 1933 wurde es als «Stadio Benito Mussolini» eröffnet und nach dem 2. Weltkrieg zum «Stadio Comunale» umbenannt, bevor es für die Olympiade 2006 seinen heutigen Namen erhielt.

own private stadium, complete with an adjacent shopping centre.

This is how things worked in Italy (and in Turin) at the dawn of the third millennium.

The Olympics in Turin: an organisational and PR success with many limitations

Everything went smoothly during the 15 days of the competitions; everyone agrees that the organisation was close to perfect. And Turin's image throughout the world was greatly enhanced. But what is the legacy of 'Torino 2006' in economic and environmental terms?

The Cesana Pariol bobsleigh track is now permanently closed. Cesana Torinese's town council unanimously decided so during the summer of 2014. Excessive operating costs and very low utilisation prospects led to the decision not to reopen the facility and to redevelop the site instead. In the meantime, the over 48 tons of ammonia of the refrigeration cycle were removed – a real environmen-

tal time bomb at high altitude. It is hard to imagine what will happen to the 19 curves of the concrete track crawling over one kilometre of meadows and larch groves. It will be difficult to restore this place to its original state. Some will recall that the project was off to a bad start: the site (chosen as a fall-back solution after another location was dropped for technical reasons) consists of a slope that is exposed to the sun, which is far from ideal for a bobsleigh track. In this respect, the attitude of the International Olympic Committee (IOC), coupled with the short-sighted nationalist pride of the organisers, was truly irresponsible: it made it impossible to consider the option of reusing the La Plagne bobsleigh track (used during the Albertville Olympics of 1992), which was not that far from the venues of the Olympic Games in Turin. The Italian organisers did not even consider the proposal worked out by environmental organisations to build temporary

1 – The biathlon shooting range in snow-covered San Sicario.

2 – The Stadio Olimpico: opened in 1933 as Stadio Benito Mussolini, it was renamed Stadio Comunale after World War II and eventually received its current name for the 2006 Olympics.

war in aller Welt angekommen. Aber was bleibt von Turin 2006 aus ökonomischer Sicht zurück? Wie sieht es mit der Umweltbelastung aus? Die Bobbahn in Cesana Pariol bleibt in Zukunft definitiv geschlossen. Der Kommunalrat von Cesana Torinese hat dies im Verlauf des Sommers 2014 einstimmig entschieden. Zu hohe Unterhaltskosten und unzureichende Auslastung haben zum Entschluss geführt, die Anlage nicht zu sanieren und die ursprünglich geplante Wiedereröffnung zu streichen. In der Zwischenzeit wurden 48 Tonnen Ammoniak aus dem Kühlkreislauf entsorgt, eine echte ökologische Bombe im Hochgebirge. Was aus dem Betonwall samt seinen 19 Kurven, der sich über mehr als einen Kilometer über Wiesen und Lärchenhaine erstreckt, wohl werden wird? Der Ort wird niemals wieder der alte sein. Einige erinnern sich daran, dass dieses Projekt bereits einen schlechten Start hatte: Das Gelände wurde aus technischen Gründen einem anderen, verlassenen Areal bevorzugt. Das auserwählte Terrain wies aber auch ein sonnendurchflutetes Teilstück auf, was einer Bobbahn nun mal nicht zuträglich ist. Die Haltung des Internationalen Olympischen Komitees (IOC), kombiniert mit dem Nationalstolz kurzsichtiger Veranstalter, war unverantwortlich, weil sie die Möglichkeit der Wiederverwendung der Bobbahn von La Plagne (Olympische Spiele Albertville 1992) nicht zuliess, obwohl diese nicht allzu weit von den Wettkampfstätten in Turin entfernt ist. Die italienischen Organisatoren ignorierten den Vorschlag der Umweltschutzorganisationen, temporäre Strukturen zu schaffen, die sie nach Ende der Veranstaltung entfernen könnten, um so die Kosten und Auswirkungen auf die Umwelt gering zu halten.

Die Bobbahn ist der augenfälligste Fehler der Olympischen Spiele in Turin – sie ist nicht nur ein Makel für die Stadt, sondern für das Land Italien, das zum wiederholten Mal unfähig war, Investitionen in Millionenhöhe sinnvoll zu nutzen. Es sollte auch an die Athleten

3 – Die Bobbahn in Cesana Pariol ist aus Kostengründen endgültig geschlossen worden.

4 – Antonio De Sanctis, Mitglied der Italienischen Bobmannschaft 2006, hoffte bis zuletzt, dass die Bahn wieder eröffnet wird.

facilities which could be removed after the event and would have been a less costly solution with a lower environmental impact.

The bobsleigh track is the most blatant stain of the Turin Olympics, a stain not only for Turin, but for all of Italy, once again incapable of making proper use of millions in investments. Let us also think about the athletes of the disciplines considered as lesser sports, who gain visibility only every four years and who are forced to train abroad. They too were disappointed, thinking that they would finally have an Italian track.

Turin, a large city in the plains, hosting the Winter Games

Gianni Agnelli, then chairman of FIAT, very much wanted to bring the 2006 Olympic Games to Turin; he made full use of his international influence to ensure that the IOC would choose the Piedmont city. It must be kept in mind that

FIAT and the Agnelli family have always shaped Turin's politics and that the city administration has always been very 'accommodating' towards FIAT. This was also true in the case of the 2006 Games. In fact, people close to FIAT, sometimes even family members with dubious qualifications in the field, were appointed to top positions in TOROC (the Torino Organising Committee) and in the Torino 2006 organising committee. TOROC was a private-law foundation and therefore not subject to the rules and supervision applying to public contracts. Originally, it managed only private resources, but when TOROC ran out of funds, its debts were covered by the public purse. On the other hand, the Torino 2006 organising committee was a government entity whose purpose was to set up the infrastructure needed for the Games financed by public funds. For this reason, it was subject to the regulations and supervision applying to public contracts.

Cost explosion, public bodies pick up the bill

After the IOC awarded the Games to Turin, a budget of about two billion euros was allocated for the event. 1.4 billion euros were to be contributed by the central government, 200 million euros by the city of Turin, 300 million euros by private sources and 159 million euros by other bodies. Revenues (television rights, sponsorship money, tickets, etc.) amounted to a little less than one billion euros. Organisational costs amounted to about 1.5 billion euros, building the facilities, in contrast, cost over two billion euros. An additional contribution from the public purse was therefore needed to cover the deficit. And yet, the application submitted in 1998 estimated costs of about 500 million euros. In the end, 3.5 billion were spent, rather than the estimated 500 million. There are always cost overruns when major projects are realised and organised, especially

dieser Disziplinen gedacht werden, Vertreter einer Randsportart, die alle vier Jahre zu Ruhm gelangen und die heute dazu gezwungen sind, im Ausland zu trainieren. Auch sie wurden in ihrer Hoffnung betrogen, endlich auf einer italienischen Bahn fahren und trainieren zu können.

Turin, eine Grossstadt im Tiefland, beherbergt die Olympischen Winterspiele

Gianni Agnelli, damaliger Präsident von Fiat, wünschte sich die Olympischen Spiele in Turin 2006 dringlich herbei. Er liess seinen ganzen Einfluss wirken, damit das IOC die piemontesische Stadt als Austragungsort auswählte. Es sei daran erinnert, dass Fiat und die Familie Agnelli seit jeher die Turiner Politik beeinflussen und sich diese schon immer fügsam gezeigt hat. Diesbezüglich hat sich auch bei den Winterspielen 2006 nichts geändert. In der Tat, auch an der Spitze des TOROC, des Organisationskomitees in Turin, und der *Agenzia Torino 2006* standen Vertrauenspersonen von Fiat, manche stammten sogar aus der Familie und ihre Eignung für die jeweilige Funktion war fragwürdig. TOROC war als Privatstiftung gegründet worden und unterlag somit weder den Vorschriften noch den Kontrollen des öffentlichen Beschaffungswesens. Die Stiftung hatte private Ressourcen zu verwenden, aber als diese Fonds aufgebraucht waren, wurden offene Forderungen durch die öffentliche Hand beglichen. Die *Agenzia Torino 2006* hingegen war ein Regierungsunternehmen mit dem Ziel, die Verwirklichung der notwendigen Infrastruktur für die Winterspiele mit öffentlichen Mitteln zu sichern. Die *Agenzia* unterlag daher den Vorschriften und Kontrollen des öffentlichen Beschaffungswesens.

5 — Die «Passerella Olimpica» verbindet in Turin das Olympische Dorf mit dem Quartier Lingotto.

in Italy. However, it should be kept in mind that when a city signs the so-called Host City Contract, it signs a one-sided contract that binds it to comply with all rules imposed by the IOC for the organisation of the Games. TOROC found itself in the situation of having to fulfil the commitments assumed by the city of Turin towards the IOC. The Olympics, as all one-time events, have irrefutable deadlines. It is (in most cases) impossible to change the original designs or to propose improvements during the implementation phase. The schedule would not allow it. A city should think twice before signing a contract with the IOC.

When dealing with a major sports event (and all that comes with it, before, during, and after), a distinction must be made between what happens in a large city like Turin and what happens in outlying mountain areas. In fact the capacity of a large city to deal with a major sports event is very different from that of

a small settlement. This becomes clear when taking a look at the sports facilities built for the Olympic events.

Massive infrastructure for two weeks of competition

Almost all sports venues that were newly built in the city of Turin to host indoor ice sports competitions could be converted to accommodate other sports, musical or cultural events. The Oval, built to host the skating competitions at a cost of about 70 million euros, was converted into a trade fair pavilion. The Palaolimpico, the ice hockey arena now called Pala Alpitour, which was built at a cost of 85 million euros, now hosts concerts, shows, and events of various kinds. These venues are in use after the Olympics without incurring a deficit because they are located in a metropolitan area serving a large population base. Things are quite different for the infrastructure that was built in the mountains. After the

3 — The Cesana Pariol bobsleigh track was permanently closed for financial reasons.

4 — Antonio De Sanctis, member of the Italian bobsled team in 2006, never gave up hope that the track would reopen.

5 — The Passerella Olimpica platform in Turin connects the Olympic Village and the Lingotto district.

Kosten schnellen in die Höhe, es zahlt die öffentliche Hand

Rund zwei Milliarden Euro betrug das Budget für die Olympischen Spiele in Turin, nachdem die Austragung durch das IOC bestätigt worden war: 1,4 Milliarden zu Lasten des Staates, 200 Millionen seitens der Verwaltung von Turin, 300 Millionen aus privater Hand und 159 Millionen aus weiteren Körperschaften. Die Einnahmen aus Fernsehrechten, Sponsoring, Tickets etc. lagen fast bei einer Milliarde Euro. Die Organisationskosten beliefen sich auf circa 1,5 Milliarden Euro, während die Umsetzung der Projekte weit mehr als zwei Milliarden Euro betrug. Um die Rechnungen zu begleichen, war folglich ein weiteres Eingreifen der öffentlichen Hand notwendig. Zur Erinnerung: Das Kandidaturdossier aus dem Jahr 1998 hatte Ausgaben von insgesamt 500 Millionen Euro veranschlagt! Schließlich wurden also 3,5 Milliarden statt 500 Millionen ausgegeben. Großprojekte oder die Organisation von Großanlässen und damit einhergehende Kostenexplosionen sind ein stets wiederkehrendes Charakteristikum Italiens. Dies ist insbesondere brisant, da eine Stadt mit der Unterzeichnung des *Host City Contract* einen Vertrag eingeht, der sie dazu verpflichtet, alle vom IOC vorgesehenen Regeln zur Organisation der Spiele zu respektieren. Das TOROC musste die Verpflichtungen erfüllen, welche die Stadt Turin gegenüber dem IOC eingegangen war. Die Umsetzung der Olympischen Spiele brachte, wie alle anderen singulären Anlässe, unverrückbare Termine mit sich. Man kann geplante Teilprojekte kaum modifizieren oder gar auf Verbesserungsmaßnahmen während der Umsetzung spekulieren. Die Zeitverhältnisse lassen dies nicht zu. Eine Stadt ist also gut beraten, die Unterzeichnung eines Vertrages mit dem IOC genau zu überdenken!

Wenn man von einer großen Sportveranstaltung redet – und auch von allen Nebenwirkungen, die ihr vorausgehen, sie begleiten und

6 – Das Gleisfeld in Turin mit Blick zum Eisschnelllaufstadion «Oval Lingotto», das heute als Messehalle genutzt wird.

Olympic events, the facilities in the mountain areas, such as those used for ski jumping or the bobsleigh competitions (disciplines that have no tradition and few active athletes in Italy and especially in the western Alps) are hardly ever used or have been abandoned altogether. The costs for building these facilities were far from negligible (35 million euros for the ski jumping hills, over 60 million euros for the bobsleigh and luge track) and the operating costs to keep them functional are not insignificant either: annual investments of 1.6 and 2.2 million, respectively, would have been necessary to keep them operational. Because of these unsustainable costs, these facilities repeatedly came close to being dismantled and were saved in extremis several times by public subsidies, only to eventually be abandoned permanently, in the case of the bobsleigh track, or almost in the case of the ski jumping hill. But these are just a few examples. The stadium that hosted the biathlon shooting range (which cost 25 million euros) also slumbers unused under the snow. Even the Olympic cross-country skiing course, in which over 20 million euros were invested, was demoted to a mere amateur trail and has not hosted any official competitions in a long time. The post-Olympic operation of the ice skating stadiums of Torre Pellice and Pinerolo (two towns at the mouths of valleys) has also been far from profitable.

The Alps are not a place for major sports events

Mountainous areas pay a price for hosting the Olympic Winter Games; and what happened in the valleys of Piedmont during the 2006 Games is proof of that. It is said that the Olympic Winter Games bring fame and resources to the host region. This is true for two weeks, perhaps.

Everyone considered them as the 'Turin Games' but the city of Turin, which was the centre of the attention of half of the world, hosted only a few indoor sports events, while most of the competitions took place in the mountains, in the upper Susa and Chisone valleys, quite far away from Turin, not only in terms of distance but also of culture and traditions. On the one hand, there is the large, formerly industrial city, on the other hand, there are the small mountain locations. Although most of the competitions were held outside Turin, the awards ceremonies were exclusively held in the very central Piazza Castello, the city's outdoor sitting room. The Olympics were a marketing and promotion opportunity for the city of Turin during the post-industrial crisis period that the city was going through.

For the politicians and organisers who strongly advocated them, the Olympics should have been an opportunity to completely revamp the rather inefficient tourism system of Piedmont's mountain areas that was based on uncontrolled development of

ihr folgen –, ist es notwendig, zwischen den Geschehnissen im Stadtzentrum von Turin und jenen in den peripheren Berggebieten zu unterscheiden. Die «Leidensfähigkeit» einer Großstadt während eines sportlichen Großanlasses ist eine andere als die eines kleineren Ballungszentrums. Diese Tatsache wird bei der Analyse der Sporteinrichtungen, die man braucht, um die Olympischen Spiele überhaupt durchzuführen, offensichtlich.

Unzählige Anlagen für gerade mal zwei Wochen Wettkampf

Die in der Stadt Turin erbauten Anlagen für die Wettkämpfe im Bereich Eissport (Indoor) wurden für andere Sportevents oder Kulturanlässe umgebaut. Die Errichtung des Ovals für die Skating-Wettbewerbe belief sich auf 70 Millionen Euro. Es ist jetzt eine Messehalle. Für das Eishockeystadion Palaolimpico (heute Pala Alpitour) wurden 85 Millionen Euro aufgewendet. Heute organisieren die Veranstalter dort Konzerte, Spektakel und Anlässe unterschiedlicher Art. Die nacholympische Nutzung dieser Anlagen ist nicht defizitär, da sie sich in einem Ballungsgebiet befinden, wo eine Vielzahl an Veranstaltungsorten für Großevents gefragt ist. Bei den Anlagen in den Berggebieten sieht die Situation anders aus. Nach Beendigung des olympischen Events wurden die Anlagen in den Berggebieten, zum Beispiel jene für den Skisprung oder die Bobanlagen, in den seltensten Fällen wiederverwendet. Manche wurden sogar komplett aufgegeben. Es handelt sich hier primär um Anlagen für Sportarten, die in den Westalpen und insbesondere in Italien keine Tradition haben und nur von wenigen Menschen ausgeübt werden. Nicht nur die Errichtungskosten der Anlagen waren bemerkenswert – 35 Millionen Euro für die Sprunganlage sowie weitere 60 Millionen für die Bob- und Schlittenbahn –, auch die Unterhaltskosten sind beträchtlich.

7 – Das Zielgelände der Skisprunganlage in Pragelato.

8 – Auch im Winter wird die neue Sprungschanze nicht genutzt.

holiday homes and weekend commuting. It was an opportunity to develop hotels, to relaunch, on the crest of the great Olympic event, high-quality tourism viable throughout the year, instead of being limited to seasonal peaks. It was said that, in the long term, even remote mountain areas not directly involved in the Games would benefit from the event. Now, eight years later, disenchantment with these promises prevails in the valleys around Turin. When taking a closer look, nothing seems to have changed: lines of cars snake their way up the mountains on weekends, Olympic villages have been converted into residences and holiday homes, there are no vacancies around New Year's time, but for the rest of the year, the mountain area around Turin is left to its own devices, with the Olympic white elephants and their ensuing costs. In the meantime, the Piedmont region has to bear the costs for generating artificial snow at the Via Lattea ski complex, the same slopes that hosted slalom and downhill champions like Rocca, Aamodt, Raich and Ligety, while Sestriere is no longer among the locations hosting World Cup competitions. The ultimate heritage the Olympics left behind for the mountain areas amounts to oversized infrastructure, high operating costs, and additional unoccupied beds. True, the road network of the Susa and Chisone valleys was greatly improved by the construction of bypasses and new roads. But these works were badly needed anyway and the fact that they had to wait for the Olympics to be finally built is not something to boast about. In any case, these projects were financed by public funds. However, the infrastructure intervention on the road system did not improve the valleys' local public transportation system. During the 15 days of the Games, an efficient transportation system made it possible to move 20,000 people per day (not including spectators) along the valleys to and from Turin. How-

6 – View of the railway tracks in Turin and the Oval Lingotto speed skating stadium, which serves as a congress centre today.

7 – The finish area of the ski-jump venue in Pragelato.

8 – The new ski jump lies idle even in winter.

Jährlich wären 1,6 beziehungsweise 2,2 Millionen Euro für die Aufrechterhaltung der Funktionstüchtigkeit notwendig gewesen. Solche Anlagen wurden bereits mehrfach aufgrund der teuren Bewirtschaftung zurückgebaut. Sie wurden auch mehrmals in letzter Minute gerettet, und zwar mit Subventionen aus öffentlicher Hand, um später definitiv geschlossen zu werden, wie wir am Beispiel der Bobbahn gesehen haben. Der Sprungturm entging diesem Schicksal nur knapp. Aber damit nicht genug. Auch das Stadion mit dem Biathlonschießstand, dessen Kosten sich auf 25 Millionen Euro beliefen, liegt unter Schneemassen und wird nicht benützt. Die olympische Langlaufpiste, für die mehr als 20 Millionen Euro ausgegeben wurden, ist zu einer touristischen Piste degradiert worden und beherbergt seit geraumer Zeit keine offiziellen Wettkämpfe mehr. Auch die Verwaltung und Bewirtschaftung der zwei Eisstadien von Torre Pellice und Pinerolo, zwei Städtchen in Talmündungen, sind alles andere als rentabel.

9 — Die Gebäude der Skisprunganlage sind nach wie vor in gutem Zustand, stehen aber leer.

Die Alpen eignen sich nicht für sportliche Grossanlässe

Olympische Winterspiele haben negative Auswirkungen auf Alpinregionen. Soviel folgern wir aus den Spielen 2006 und ihren Effekten in den Tälern des Piemonts. Es heißt, die Olympischen Winterspiele bringen den Gastgeberregionen Ansehen und Ressourcen. Das ist korrekt, doch hält der Ruhm genau zwei Wochen an.

Alle hielten die Spiele 2006 für die «Spiele von Turin», aber die Stadt Turin, auf der die Augen der halben Welt ruhten, beherbergte nur einige wenige Indoor-Sportarten, während der Großteil der Wettkämpfe sich in den Berggebieten abspielte, in den Hochtälern Susa und Chisone, weit von Turin entfernt. Und das nicht nur physisch, sondern auch auf kultureller und traditioneller Ebene.

ever, once the event was over, and even now, eight years later, reaching the mountain locations of the Susa and Chisone valleys by public transport continues to be a true feat, both for tourists and residents. But, as we all know, in the case of major events, everything is meant to work only for the time of the event itself. After the curtain falls, the TV lights go off, and athletes and journalists leave, everything returns to how it was and the change brought about by the event and the waste of millions of euros do not mean much.

A misinformed public

Public opinion was greatly influenced by the mass media – which are controlled by political and business lobbies in Italy – which emphasised only the positive aspects. In other cities such as Munich and Salzburg and other locations such as the canton of Grisons, Valle d'Aosta, and Val Gardena, the population was invited to express its opinion in referenda and had the chance to oppose the possibility of hosting Olympic Games. However, it is likely that even if a referendum had been held in Turin, a majority of the population would have been in favour. The mountain municipalities – small communities with limited potential to influence the strategic choices made in Rome and Turin – went along believing that they would get their share of the 'pie'. There was little opposition to the Turin Games in the form of a 'No Olympics' citizens' committee and environmental organisations, because almost the entire national press, not to mention Turin's press controlled by FIAT and the Agnelli family, were in favour of the Games. The environmental organisations took an approach of no compromises, even after the Games were awarded to Turin, rather than trying to limit the damage by improving the projects with the strongest environmental impact and unsustainable costs. The result was an ineffective and un-

successful strategy. Even the few mayors of the mountain municipalities that were not in favour capitulated eventually, perhaps fearing that they would be denied their share of the Olympic 'pie'. Now everyone has their share… including a share of the debts.

Hosting the Olympic Games again?

Today Turin, as all cities that have hosted the Olympic Games, is struggling with heavy debts. The heritage left by 'Torino 2006' is a deficit of over 300 million euros, including the deficit of the TOROC budget and the loss generated by the Olympic facilities. In 2001 the city's overall debt amounted to about 1.7 billion euros; by 2007, it had grown to almost three billion and to almost 4.5 billion in 2012. A large part, although not all of it, is due to the expansion of the underground system and to the various urban renewal projects built in support of the Olympic events. 'Do London a favour: give

Einerseits die große, ehemals industrielle Stadt, andererseits die kleinen Ortschaften in den Berggebieten. Für die Stadt Turin war es, in einer Zeit der postindustriellen Krise, eine Marketing- und Werbemaßnahme, auch wenn der Löwenanteil der Turniere anderswo stattfand. Bemerkenswert ist, dass alle Feierlichkeiten und Preisverleihungen rigoros und ohne Ausnahme in der zentral gelegenen Piazza Castello, dem «Stadtsalon», durchgeführt wurden.

Für die Politiker und Organisatoren, die sich die Olympischen Spiele herbeigewünscht hatten, waren sie eine letztendlich nicht genutzte Gelegenheit, das touristische Konzept für die Urlaubsorte der Region Piemont (unkontrollierte Entwicklung von Zweitwohnungen und endlose Pendlerfahrtzeiten an den Wochenenden) komplett neu und zu eigenen Gunsten zu definieren. Man hätte Hotelbetten schaffen, nach dem Großanlass eine Qualitätsoffensive im Tourismus lancieren und auf ein langfristiges Konzept setzen müssen, anstatt sich weiterhin auf wenige saisonale Spitzenzeiten zu beschränken. Es hieß sogar, dass auf lange Sicht auch die peripheren Berggebiete, die nicht von den Spielen beeinflusst worden waren, von der Veranstaltung profitieren sollten. Heute, acht Jahre danach, hat sich in den Tälern rund um Turin Ernüchterung in Bezug auf diese Versprechen breitgemacht. Bei genauerer Betrachtung hat sich gar nichts geändert: Autoschlangen am Wochenende, Olympische Dörfer, die in Wohnsitze und Zweitwohnungen umgewandelt wurden, nur zu Jahresende ausgebuchte Quartiere – den Rest des Jahres ist die Berglandschaft um Turin, samt ihren olympischen Kathedralen und den entsprechenden Bewirtschaftungskosten, verwaist. In der Zwischenzeit hat die Region Piemont sich die Kosten der künstlichen Beschneiung des Skigebiets Via Lattea auferlegt, und zwar jener Pisten, auf denen Slalom- und Abfahrt-Champions wie Rocca, Aamondt, Raich und Ligety fuhren. Sestriere wurde hingegen aus der Liste der Ortschaf-

10 — Die Bobbahn in Cesana Pariol von der Seilbahn aus gesehen.

the Olympics to Paris.' This spontaneous comment was made by the *Economist* in May 2008, at the time of the presentation of the cities (London, Paris, Moscow, Madrid, and New York) vying to host the 2008 Olympics. Hosting the Olympics is becoming increasingly less attractive to Western democratic countries. This is supported by the fact that in the most recent past, the Olympics were awarded to an emerging country like South Korea (2018) or to a country ruled by a populist regime, like Putin's Russia (Sochi), and that China and Kazakhstan are competing for the 2022 Games after Norway withdrew.

And yet, at this time, right in the middle of the *Mafia Capitale* scandal, following the discovery of corruption among politicians and officials in the municipality of Rome, the Italian government has announced the candidature of Rome for the 2024 Summer Olympics. It looks as if the lesson has not been learned…

9 — The buildings of the ski-jump venue are still in good shape, but remain empty.

10 — The bobsleigh track in Cesana Pariol seen from the cableway.

ten gestrichen, die Weltmeisterschaftswettkämpfe austragen. Am Ende bedeutet das olympische Erbe für die Wintersportorte nichts anderes als überdimensionierte Infrastruktur, hohe Betriebskosten und noch mehr leere Betten. Zugegeben, das Straßennetz des Berggebietes der Täler Susa und Chisone hat durch den Bau neuer Straßen und Umfahrungen deutliche Verbesserungen erfahren. Dies geschah jedoch durch öffentliche Mittel. Die Infrastrukturarbeiten auf den Straßen haben leider das System des öffentlichen Nahverkehrs in den Tälern nicht verbessert. Ermöglichte ein effizientes Verkehrssystem während der 15 Tage der Winterspiele es täglich über 20 000 Menschen (die Zuschauermassen noch nicht mitgerechnet), sich aus den Tälern nach Turin und zurück zu bewegen, ist es heute, acht Jahre nach den Olympischen Spielen, sowohl für Touristen als auch für die Anwohner weiterhin ein umständliches Unterfangen, die Skiorte im Susa- und im Chisonetal mit öffentlichen Verkehrsmitteln zu erreichen. Es ist klar, während des Großereignisses tut man alles, um die Erreichbarkeit der wesentlichen Austragungsorte sicherzustellen. Wenn der Vorhang fällt, die Sportler und Journalisten den Veranstaltungsort verlassen haben und alles zur Normalität zurückkehrt, ist es egal, wie stark ein Gebiet durchgerüttelt wurde und wie viele Millionen Euro in den Wind geworfen wurden.

Getäuschte Bevölkerung

Die öffentliche Meinung war stark von den Massenmedien beeinflusst, die ausschließlich die positiven Aspekte zeigten. Die Medien in Italien werden von den politischen und wirtschaftlichen Lobbys gesteuert. In anderen Städten wie München, Salzburg, im Kanton Graubünden, im Aostatal und im Val Gardena konnten die Menschen in einer Volksbefragung ihre Meinung kundtun. Sie hatten die Chance, gegen die Ausrichtung von Winterspielen zu stimmen. Eine Mehrheit der Bürger von Turin hätte sich bei einem Referendum aber wohl dafür ausgesprochen.

Die Berggemeinden, kleine Gemeinden mit begrenzten Möglichkeiten, Rom und Turin zu beeinflussen, haben sich in ihr Schicksal gefügt, nicht zuletzt, um bei der Aufteilung des Kuchens finanziell beteiligt zu werden.

Der Widerstand gegen die Winterspiele in Turin war auf einen Ausschuss von Bürgern unter dem Motto «Nein zu den Olympischen Spielen» sowie die Proteste von Umweltschutzorganisationen begrenzt. Es war schwierig, sich Gehör zu verschaffen, da die nationale Presse geschlossen hinter den Spielen stand und speziell die Medien aus Turin komplett in der Hand von Fiat und der Familie Agnelli sind. Die Umweltschutzorganisationen wollten jedoch auch nach der Vergabe der Spiele an Turin die Projekte mit dem gravierendsten Einfluss auf die Umwelt und den exorbitantesten Kosten verbessern, anstatt sich bloss auf eine Begrenzung des Schadens zu konzentrieren – eine Strategie, de facto gegen alle zu kämpfen. Sie entpuppte sich als unwirksam. Auch die weniger überzeugten Bürgermeister der Berggemeinden – einsame Kämpfer – kapitulierten schließlich, vielleicht aus Angst, bei der Aufteilung des «olympischen Kuchens» ausgeschlossen zu werden. So erhielt jeder Einzelne ein Stück davon, auch vom Schuldenberg.

Die Olympischen Spiele nochmals ausrichten?

Turin hat sich schwer verschuldet, wie fast alle Veranstaltungsorte der Olympischen Spiele. Das Erbe der Winterspiele 2006 sind 300 Millionen Euro an Budgetdefizit, wenn man auch die Löcher im Etat des TOROC und die Verluste der heute unbenutzten Anlagen berücksichtigt. Im Jahr 2001 hatte die Stadt eine Gesamtverschuldung von rund 1,7 Milliarden Euro, im Jahr 2007 sind die Schulden auf fast drei und bis 2012 auf 4,5 Milliarden angestiegen. Verursacht wurden diese Schulden zum Großteil durch die Erweiterung des U-Bahn-Netzes

und andere Stadtsanierungsprojekte, die im Zuge der olympischen
Veranstaltungen realisiert wurden. «Tut London einen Gefallen und
überlasst Paris die Veranstaltung der Olympischen Spiele.» So ein
Kommentar im britischen Economist vom Mai 2004 bezüglich der Veröf-
fentlichung der Bewerberstädte für die Olympischen Spiele im Jahr
2008 – London, Paris, Moskau, Madrid und New York. Für ein westliches,
demokratisches Land werden die Olympischen Spiele immer weniger
interessant. Tatsächlich vergibt das IOC die Spiele aktuell an
Schwellenländer wie Korea (2018) oder Nationen mit populistischen
Regimes wie Putins Russland (Sotschi 2014). Für 2022 konnten sich
China und Kasachstan durchsetzen, nachdem sich Norwegen gerade
noch zurückziehen konnte. Ende 2014 hat die italienische Regierung
die Kandidatur Roms für die Olympischen Sommerspiele 2024 ange-
kündigt, während gleichzeitig ein Skandal um die *Mafia Capitale* und
die Aufdeckung korrupter Politiker und Beamter in der Verwaltung
der Stadt Rom Aufsehen erregte. Offenbar war uns das bisherige
olympische Erlebnis noch nicht Lehre genug.

Der Ingenieur Francesco Pastorelli ist Direktor der
CIPRA Italia (italienische Sektion der Internationalen
Alpenschutzkommission). In dieser Funktion hat
er die Ereignisse in Turin 2006 verfolgt, von der
Kandidatur bis zum heutigen Tag, mit spezifischem
Augenmerk auf die Bergregionen. Bei CIPRA Italia
befasst er sich mit Umweltfragen der Alpenregion
und mit nachhaltigen Entwicklungsmodellen für die
Berggemeinden. Francesco Pastorelli lebt in Turin
und in Carnino, einer kleinen Gemeinde im oberen
Tanarotal, wo er aufgewachsen ist.

Francesco Pastorelli, engineer by training, is the
director of CIPRA Italia (the Italian chapter of
the International Commission for the Protection of
the Alps). In this capacity, he followed the events
of 'Torino 2006', from the candidature up to today,
paying special attention to the issue of mountainous regions. Within CIPRA Italia, he covers topics
concerning the alpine environment and sustainable
mountain development models. Through CIPRA,
an international NGO represented in seven alpine
countries, he participates in round tables and
international networks involved in the various
sectors of sustainable mountain development. He
divides his time between Turin and Carnino, a small
hamlet in Alta Valle Tanaro, where he grew up.

«Passerella Olimpica» in Turin
The Passerella Olimpica in Turin

Das Olympische Dorf in Turin wird auch als Asylunterkunft genutzt
The Olympic Village in Turin is also used for refugee housing

Teile des Olympischen Dorfes wurden zu Markthallen umgenutzt
Parts of the Olympic Village were transformed into indoor markets

Eisschnelllaufstadion vom Dach der ehemaligen Fiat-Fabrik «Lingotto» aus gesehen
The speed skating stadium seen from the roof of the former FIAT factory Lingotto 128

Eisstadion «Palavela» in Turin
The Palavela ice stadium in Turin

Eisstadion «Palavela»
The Palavela ice stadium

«Stadio Olimpico», die Heimspielstätte des Torino FC
The Stadio Olimpico, the home arena of Torino FC

Schießstand der Biathlonanlage in San Sicario
Shooting range of the biathlon facilities in San Sicario

Hotel «Olympic Centre» neben der Biathlonschießanlage
The Olympic Centre Hotel adjacent to the biathlon facilities

Im Innern der Bobbahn in Cesana Pariol
Inside the bobsleigh track at Cesana Pariol

Gelände der Bobbahn in Cesana Pariol
The premises of the bobsleigh track in Cesana Pariol

Anzeigetafel im Zielgelände der Bobbahn
Scoreboard in the finish area of the bobsleigh track

Skisprunganlage in Pragelato
Ski-jump venue in Pragelato

«Pragelato Ski Jumping Hotel»: auch in der Hochsaison geschlossen
The Pragelato Ski Jumping Hotel: also closed in the peak season

Zwei Skisprungschanzen mit dazugehörigem Lift
Two ski jumps including lifts

Jurorenhaus und Flutlichtanlage der Skisprungschanzen
The judges tower and floodlights of the ski jumps

14

PEKING 2008
OLYMPISCHE SOMMERSPIELE

Die Spiele des «falschen» Lächelns

Essay von Barbara Lüthi

BEIJING 2008
SUMMER OLYMPICS

The Games of the 'Fake' Smile

Essay by Barbara Lüthi

Die Transformation einer Stadt

2006 zog ich nach Peking. Die düster wirkende Hauptstadt eines nominal noch kommunistischen Landes, die aussah wie ein Provisorium und sich anhörte wie eine gigantische Baustelle. Die größte Nation der Welt befand sich in der wohl dramatischsten Umbruchsphase ihrer Geschichte und die Hauptstadt bereitete sich auf die Olympischen Spiele vor. Es sollten Spiele der Superlative werden. China wollte die besten, teuersten und modernsten Spiele aller Zeiten präsentieren.

Für diese gigantische Selbstinszenierung verschwanden große Teile der Stadt und wurden neu aufgebaut. Damit entstand ein berauschendes Gefühl der Wandlungsfähigkeit. Die Transformation der Stadt war kompromisslos. So wurden beispielsweise die Hutongs, die traditionellen Hofhäuser, abgerissen, um Platz zu machen für Monumente der Modernisierung: futuristische TV-Türme, Bürobauten aus Beton, Stadien aus Stahl und ein neuer Flughafenterminal, der Peking mit der Welt verbinden sollte. Die Schnelligkeit dieser Veränderung trieb alles ins Extreme, oft war die Stadt vollends in dichten Smog eingehüllt, die Baukräne ragten gespenstisch aus dem milchigen Dunst. Es sah aus, als würde die Welt untergehen, doch in Wirklichkeit wurde sie neu erschaffen.

Doch bei aller Euphorie gab es auch Kritik. Die groß angelegte Zwangsumsiedlung von Tausenden von Bürgern in die Vorstädte Pekings erregte Aufsehen. Es lohne sich nicht, die Hutongs zu renovieren, begründete die Stadtregierung die Abrissprogramme. Wo an einem Tag Restaurants, Geschäfte und Häuser standen, waren am nächsten Tag nur noch Trümmerhaufen zu sehen. Ich treffe Ding Jie inmitten einer Trümmerwüste. Ihr traditionelles Haus, in dem ihre Familie seit Generationen lebt, ist eines der wenigen, das noch

1 — Eine brachliegende Fläche nördlich des «Nationalstadions» in Peking.

2 — Der Olympiapark ist eine Attraktion, vor allem auch für chinesische Touristen.

The transformation of a city

In 2006, I moved to Beijing, the gloomy capital of an — at least on paper — still Communist country that looked like a provisional arrangement and sounded like a colossal construction site. The world's largest nation was in the midst of what was likely the most dramatic period of transition in its history and the capital was getting ready for the Olympic Games. And nothing short of superlative would do. China was determined to host the best, most expensive and modern Games of all times.

To this end, large parts of the city were demolished, only to be rebuilt as part of this gigantic show. In the wake of these activities, the feeling of enabling change was intoxicating. No compromises were made in the transformation of the city. The *hutongs*, the traditional courtyard residences, for instance, were knocked down to make room for monuments of modernisation: futuristic TV towers, concrete office buildings, stadiums made of steel and a new airport terminal to connect Beijing to the world. The rapid pace of this change pushed everything to the extreme: many times the city was veiled in thick clouds of smog, construction cranes eerily protruding from the milky haze. The world seemed to end while in reality, it was being created anew.

But there were some critical voices piercing the general mood of euphoria. The numerous forced evictions that edged thousands of citizens into Beijing's suburbs did not go unnoticed. The city government defended its demolition programme, saying it would be uneconomical to renovate the *hutongs*. Restaurants, shops and houses disappeared over night to be replaced by heaps of rubble. I meet Ding Jie in the middle of a rubble desert. The traditional house in which her family has lived for generations is among the few still standing in the historic Qianmen quarter. 'Nobody wants to leave this place', says Ding Jie.

'The government wants us to move, but the *hutongs* and the people living in them belong together. There is no place else where we could live in such harmony again.'

The old city is demolished in record time, two thirds of Beijing's historic centre have already vanished. By early 2006, Beijing's construction zone has expanded over 50 million square metres. A gigantic business endeavour, for federal land rights can be purchased. The authorities lease them to the real estate companies that pay the highest price.

Over night, posters announcing the dates of demolition appear on house walls. According to the houses' inhabitants, objections are useless. The bulldozers appear on schedule and in the worst-case scenario, people only have 24 hours to pack their belongings. This is the fate of Ms Zhou, who leads me through her *hutong,* which is scheduled to be demolished the next day. 'I don't know where to go. They want to take my life', the old woman says, weeping.

steht im historischen Qianmen-Viertel. «Niemand will hier weg», sagt Ding Jie. «Die Regierung möchte, dass wir umziehen, doch die Hutongs und die Menschen, die in den Hutongs wohnen, bilden eine Einheit. Nirgends sonst können wir wieder ein solch harmonisches Umfeld finden.»

Die Altstadt wird in Rekordzeit abgerissen, zwei Drittel des historischen Pekings sind bereits verschwunden. Anfang 2006 misst Pekings Bauzone 50 Millionen Quadratmeter. Ein gigantisches Business, denn staatliche Bodenrechte sind käuflich, sie werden von den Behörden an jene Immobilienfirmen verpachtet, die am meisten bezahlen.

In der Nacht werden Plakate an die Hauswand geklebt, die verkünden, wann es zum Abriss kommen soll. Laut den Hausbewohnern nützen Einsprachen nichts. Die Bulldozer kommen pünktlich und den Menschen bleiben im schlimmsten Fall nur 24 Stunden, um zu packen. So wie Frau Zhou, die mich durch ihren Hutong führt, der am nächsten Tag abgerissen werden soll. «Ich weiß nicht, wo ich hin soll. Sie wollen mir mein Leben wegnehmen», weint die alte Frau.

Frau Zhou zeigt uns den Vertrag, den sie unterschreiben musste, falls sie eine Kompensation erhalten will. Wie hoch diese ist und wo sie das Geld abholen kann, darüber wurde die alte Frau nicht informiert.

Laut den Behörden wurde eine Entschädigungssumme pro Quadratmeter festgelegt, doch genaue Zahlen möchte uns das Büro für Stadtplanung nicht geben. Bei den Zwangsumsiedlungen fehlen geregelte Verfahren, es gib keine Mitsprache, die Fristen sind extrem kurz und die finanzielle Kompensation ist oft lächerlich klein, falls überhaupt eine bezahlt wird. Die Bürger werden oft gezwungen, in Gegenden zu ziehen, die weit weg von ihrer Gemeinschaft und ihren Arbeitsplätzen liegen. Die Vertreibung führt daher häufig zum Zerfall

3 — Im Waldstück des Mountainbikegeländes «Laoshan» haben es sich Pensionäre gemütlich eingerichtet.

Ms Zhou shows us the contract she had to sign to receive compensation. She was neither informed about the amount she would receive nor where she could collect the money.

According to the authorities, a certain compensation sum was fixed per square metre, but the municipal urban planning commission is reluctant to name figures. The forced relocations are carried out without the proper procedures; the affected persons have no say in the matter, are informed on short notice, and where financial compensation is available, it is ridiculously low. Many citizens are forced to move to neighbourhoods far away from their original communities and jobs. As a consequence, the expulsion often leads to the deterioration of social networks and, in some cases, poverty. A study by the Geneva-based human rights organisation COHRE found that in the past 20 years, more than two million people worldwide have been relocated by the organisers of Olympic Games. At

1.25 million forced evictions under the banner of the Olympic rings, China is at the spearhead of this list. Yet forced relocations in China are not only carried out for the sake of mega events. For the Chinese government, this coercive measure is a commonly used instrument of spatial planning. Many people would have been relocated sooner or later anyway. The Olympic Games in Beijing only accelerated and enforced the process.

Growing nationalism

Modern office buildings, sophisticated shopping centres and huge apartment complexes – that's what China wants the world to see. Especially the younger Chinese view the Olympic Games as an opportunity. 'Beijing has changed, it has become very modern. The world will see the city's most beautiful side', a young man says enthusiastically. 'We had to wait for the Olympic Games for 100 years. The first time we applied

1 — An unused area north of the National Stadium in Beijing.

2 — The Olympic Park is a popular sight, especially for Chinese tourists.

3 — Pensioners have found themselves a cosy spot in the woods of the Laoshan Mountain Bike Course.

sozialer Netzwerke und kann in Armut enden. Weltweit wurden in den letzten 20 Jahren über zwei Millionen Menschen von olympischen Veranstaltern umgesiedelt, lautet das Ergebnis einer Untersuchung der Menschenrechtsorganisation COHRE in Genf. Mit 1,25 Millionen Zwangsumsiedlungen im Zeichen der Ringe führt China diese Liste an. Dabei stehen in China Zwangsumsiedlungen nicht zwingend im Zusammenhang mit Großanlässen. Die chinesische Regierung bedient sich dieser Zwangsmaßnahme als ein gängiges Entwicklungsinstrument. So wären viele Menschen ohnehin umgesiedelt worden. Doch die Pekinger Spiele haben diesen Prozess beschleunigt und verstärkt.

Wachsender Nationalismus

Moderne Bürogebäude, mondäne Einkaufszentren und riesige Wohnkomplexe, das soll die Welt sehen. Vor allem junge Chinesen sehen in den Olympischen Spielen eine Chance. «Peking hat sich verändert, alles ist so modern geworden. Wir werden uns der Welt von unserer besten Seite zeigen», frohlockt ein junger Mann. «100 Jahre mussten wir auf die Olympischen Spiele warten. 1907 haben wir uns das erste Mal beworben. Jetzt ist unser Traum wahr geworden. Wir sind glücklich, China hat es geschafft, wir sind eine stolze Nation», höre ich von einem anderen Bürger der Hauptstadt.

Und es ist dieser Stolz, den die kommunistische Regierung nutzt. Das ständig präsente Gefühl des Nationalismus fand ein Ventil in einigen Ereignissen vor den Olympischen Spielen, die China schwer erzürnten: die tibetischen Aufstände und die internationalen Proteste gegen die chinesische Tibet-Politik während des olympischen Fackellaufs. Mit den Olympischen Spielen im Sommer 2008 nahm das Gefühl des Nationalismus nochmals zu. China holte die meisten Goldmedaillen, die Fans und Touristen waren mehrheitlich chinesisch.

4 — Der Olympiapark wird professionell vermarktet und zieht viele Touristen an.

for them was in 1907. Now our dream has come true. We are happy, China has made it, we are a proud nation', another citizen of the capital tells me.

And the Communist government banks on this pride. The ubiquitous feeling of nationalism found an outlet in some incidents prior to the Olympic Games that left the country furious with anger: the Tibetan uprisings and international protests against China's politics regarding Tibet during the Olympic torch relay. The 2008 Summer Olympics caused another nationalist surge. China won the most gold medals, the majority of fans and tourists were Chinese.

Yu Jie, bestselling author of more than 30 books and one of the most widely known democracy activists in China, compares the Olympic Games in Beijing to the 1936 Summer Olympics held in Germany. 'It's pure propaganda, the government calls out to the people and the world: behold what we have accomplished, we should continue ruling the country.

The Olympic Games are used by the government to further nationalism, they are a demonstration of power of a totalitarian state.'

During our interview in a restaurant on the outskirts of the city, a black Audi parks at some distance. It's the country's security agency. Before and during the Games, Yu Jie was under surveillance and admonished to refrain from meeting foreign journalists. The government also imposed restraints on other dissidents and intellectuals critical of the regime. Some were put under house arrest, held by the authorities or brought outside of the city.

Training methods are a state secret

The government had very specific ideas about what foreign journalists should report on. We were to write about China winning gold medals and the country's rapid ascent towards the top of the world. Before the Games, it was

fairly simple to get a journalist visa because the government wanted us in the country as witnesses to document China's rise.

In January 2007, a year before the Olympic Games, things changed: foreign journalists no longer had to obtain the authorities' permission for every trip and every interview. We could move around the country freely and only had to get our interview partner's consent for a talk. At the same time, the local authorities frequently made reporting difficult. On top of the correspondents already located in China, another 25,000 foreign journalists travelled to Beijing. In hosting the Olympic Games, China had, at least in theory, committed to guaranteeing the freedom of the press, one of the principles of the Olympic Charter. This Charter was violated before and during the Games: Internet access was restricted and reporting outside of the Olympic zone was even more difficult than was normally already the case. In reality, there was no

Yu Jie, Bestsellerautor von über 30 Büchern und einer der prominentesten Demokratiekämpfer in China, vergleicht die Olympischen Spiele in Peking mit den Spielen 1936 in Deutschland. «Es ist pure Propaganda, die Regierung zeigt dem Volk und der Welt: Schaut her, das haben wir alles geschaffen, wir sollten weiterregieren. Die Olympischen Spiele werden von der Regierung genutzt, um den Nationalismus zu fördern, es ist eine Machtdemonstration eines totalitären Staates.»

Während unseres Interviews in einem Restaurant am Rande der Stadt parkt in einiger Entfernung ein schwarzer Audi. Es sind die Männer der Staatssicherheit. Yu Jie stand vor und während der Spiele unter Beobachtung, ausländische Journalisten sollte er nicht treffen. Auch andere regimekritische Intellektuelle und Dissidenten wurden von der Regierung abgeschirmt. Einige wurden unter Hausarrest gestellt, festgenommen oder aus der Stadt gebracht.

Trainingsmethoden sind Staatsgeheimnis

Die Regierung hatte ganz klare Vorstellungen, worüber ausländische Journalisten berichten sollten. Wir sollten zeigen, wie China Goldmedaillen holt und wie sich das Reich in Riesenschritten an die Weltspitze bewegt. Vor den Spielen war es relativ einfach, ein Journalistenvisum zu kriegen, denn die Regierung wollte uns im Land haben: als Zeitzeugen, die Chinas Aufstieg dokumentieren.

Im Januar 2007, ein Jahr vor den Olympischen Spielen, gab es eine Veränderung: Ausländische Journalisten mussten nicht mehr für jede Reise und jedes Interview eine staatliche Bewilligung einholen. Wir konnten uns frei im Land bewegen und brauchten für Interviews nur die Einwilligung der Interviewpartner. Trotzdem wurden wir von den Lokalbehörden oft an unserer Arbeit gehindert. Zu den in China

5 — Die Sportuniversität in Peking wurde für die Spiele (2008) mit einem neuen Studentenwohnheim und einem riesigen Trainingszentrum erweitert. Der Aufwand hat sich gelohnt, China hat mit 51 Goldmedaillen die Olympiade dominiert.

such thing as freedom of the press. The Chinese government sought to make sure that an exclusively positive image of China was conveyed. Shortly before the Games started, state security officers searched our offices for sensitive film material.

The Chinese athletes were also a big taboo. As host nation, China had the biggest Olympic team. Many of the contestants were among the world leaders in their disciplines – expectations were accordingly high. Training methods are a national secret in China. Winning gold medals is a political matter. The Chinese athletes were under so much pressure that in early 2008, the government imposed a media ban on all of them. Foreign journalists thus had no way of speaking to them at all. The only exceptions were the rare press conferences with some superstars. Yao Ming, the basketball hero, told the international press in Beijing shortly before the Games: 'These Olympic Games are the biggest

opportunity in my life. But they are also a source of immense pressure. We have to be able to handle the pressure and the honour.' Pressure and honour are also elements of Chou Tao's tale. The rhythmic gymnast scored a silver medal in 2008. Six years after the Summer Games, she reminisces about the mega event. Chou has been a professional athlete since she turned ten and has been dreaming about competing in the Olympic Games for just as long. 'My family did not pressure me too much; I did that myself. And of course my trainer had tremendous expectations. But that's the only way we can use our full potential. Everyone expected us to have a breakthrough and win a medal while the Olympic Games were held in our country.'

The Games of the 'fake' smile

The Chinese government left nothing to chance. Every detail of the event was meticulously planned and executed. 25,000 security

4 — Thanks to its professional marketing the Olympic Park attracts many tourists.

5 — For the 2008 Olympics, the Beijing Sport University was extended by a new student dormitory and a gigantic training centre. The investment has paid off: with 51 gold medals, China dominated the Olympic Games.

stationierten Korrespondenten kamen weitere 25 000 ausländische Journalisten nach Peking. China hatte sich mit der Organisation der Olympischen Spiele eigentlich verpflichtet, Pressefreiheit zu garantieren. Zumindest nach außen hin, denn die Pressefreiheit ist ein Grundsatz der Olympischen Charta. Doch diese wurde auch vor und während der Spiele untergraben, denn der Internetzugang wurde nicht vollständig gewährt und das Berichten ausserhalb der olympischen Zone war noch schwieriger als sonst. Von freier Berichterstattung konnte nicht die Rede sein. Die chinesische Regierung wollte ein ausschließlich positives Chinabild vermittelt haben. Kurz vor den Olympischen Spielen wurden unsere Büros von den Beamten der Staatssicherheit nach sensiblem Filmmaterial durchsucht.

Ein Tabuthema waren auch die chinesischen Sportler. Als Gastgebernation stellte China die meisten Athleten. Viele von ihnen gehören in ihren Disziplinen zur Weltspitze – entsprechend groß waren die Erwartungen. Trainingsmethoden sind in China Staatsgeheimnis. Goldmedaillen zu gewinnen ist eine politische Angelegenheit. Der Druck auf die chinesischen Sportler war so hoch, dass die Regierung Anfang 2008 für alle chinesischen Athleten eine Mediensperre erlassen hatte. Somit war der Zugang für ausländische Journalisten unmöglich. Die Ausnahme waren die seltenen Pressekonferenzen der Superstars. Yao Ming, der Basketballstar, sagte kurz vor den Spielen vor der internationalen Presse in Peking: «Diese Olympischen Spiele sind die größte Chance meines Lebens. Aber es bedeutet auch einen unheimlichen Druck. Wir müssen mit dem Druck und mit der Ehre umgehen können.» Von dem großen Druck und der Ehre erzählt auch Chou Tao, die 2008 eine Silbermedaille in rhythmischer Gymnastik holte. Sechs Jahre nach den Sommerspielen blickt sie auf das Großereignis zurück. Seit ihrem zehnten Lebensjahr ist Chou professionelle Athletin und ebenso lange träumte sie davon, an den Olym-

6 — Die Teamleaderin der chinesischen Sportgymnastikgruppe von 2008, Chou Tao, auf dem Areal des Olympiaparks in Peking.

people were on duty to prevent turmoil. To enter Beijing, you had to show your passport before getting even close to the city. Trucks were searched. 250,000 volunteers were positioned throughout the city to report suspicious observations and assist tourists. Taxi drivers received a crash course in English, restaurants offered English menus and hordes of retirees were trained to cheer the athletes on in the stadium in a 'civilised' way. 'Ho ho – China go.' Thus went the popular slogan. Millions of trees were planted throughout the city, flower arrangements adorned every street corner. Strictly enforced driving bans markedly reduced the number of cars on the streets, six new underground and 34 new bus lines were established. The costs of the new infrastructure, construction of the gigantic sports venues and organisation of the event amounted to at least 40 billion US dollars.

One person who questioned the mega event in principle was Ai Weiwei. I interviewed the world-famous artist before the Olympic Games. He had designed the Olympic stadium, the impressive, multiple-award-winning National Stadium affectionately called Bird's Nest, in cooperation with the Swiss architect duo Herzog & de Meuron. Ai Weiwei stated dryly that he would not participate in the opening ceremony on 8 August 2008 because of the political situation in China. 'No democracy, no civil rights, a lack of equality and justice, only betrayal and treason.' The artist found nothing but words of criticism for his home country, saying he was opposed to Olympic Games under whose banner human rights violations were committed – for instance by forcing migrant workers to leave the city for the duration of the event. The Games were like a 'fake smile' for the sake of the foreigners, he said. Culture was abused for propaganda purposes.

The opening ceremony's choreography was spectacular. The Communist Party used the stage to gloriously present itself to the world and legitimate its claim to power in front of its own people. The celebration marked the temporary highlight of an impressive development that had started its course 30 years ago when China had begun to open up to business relations with the West. Eighty heads of state and government travelled to Beijing for the celebration. Never before had as many political rulers from all over the world attended the opening ceremony of Olympic Games. Only a few months prior to this moment, the Western world, indignant about the way the revolts in Tibet were suppressed in March 2008, had been considering a boycott.

The 2008 Olympic Summer Games entered the annals of history as the games of superlatives. At the same time, the Olympic idea, which is also a commitment to human rights, was seriously called into question in Beijing. The West criticised the practices of imprisoning dissidents, exploiting construction workers, steam-

pischen Spielen teilzunehmen. «Meine Familie hat mich nicht zu sehr unter Druck gesetzt, den habe ich mir selbst gemacht. Und natürlich hat mein Trainer riesigen Druck ausgeübt. Doch nur so können wir auch unser ganzes Potenzial nutzen. Alle haben erwartet, dass wir den Durchbruch schaffen und eine Medaille gewinnen, während der Olympischen Spiele in unserem Heimatland.»

Die Spiele des «falschen» Lächelns

Die chinesische Regierung überliess nichts dem Zufall. Die Spiele wurden minutiös geplant und perfekt durchgeführt. 25 000 Sicherheitsleute waren im Einsatz, um Unruhen zu vermeiden. Wer nach Peking wollte, musste weit ausserhalb der Stadt seinen Pass zeigen, Lastwagen wurden durchsucht. 250 000 freiwillige Helfer waren in der Stadt verteilt, um Verdächtiges zu melden und den Touristen zur Seite zu stehen. Taxifahrer erhielten einen Englisch-Schnellkurs, Restaurants führten Speisekarten mit englischer Übersetzung und Rentner wurden in Scharen trainiert, um in den Stadien «zivilisiert» zu jubeln und die Athleten anzufeuern. «Ho ho – China go» war der beliebteste Slogan. In der Stadt wurden Millionen von Bäumen gepflanzt, Blumenbouquets schmückten jede Straßenkreuzung. Durch strikte Fahrverbote wurde die Zahl der Autos auf den Straßen markant reduziert, es entstanden sechs neue Metro- und 34 neue Buslinien. Die Kosten für die neue Infrastruktur, den Bau der gigantischen Sportstätten und die Organisation betrugen mindestens 40 Milliarden Dollar.

Einer, der diesen Mega-Event grundsätzlich infrage stellte, war Ai Weiwei. Ich interviewte den international bekannten Künstler im Vorfeld der Olympischen Spiele. Gemeinsam mit den Schweizer Architekten Herzog & de Meuron hatte er das Olympiastadion entworfen:

7 — Ein Erinnerungsfoto vor dem «Nationalstadion» in Peking ist ein begehrtes Touristensouvenir.

rolling entire residential neighbourhoods and censuring the media. Today, the Chinese react very sensitively to the West pointing a finger in an all-encompassing sweep. The Olympic Games in Beijing showed that China was no longer willing to accept the dominating role of the West. China had already embarked on its journey to modernisation and Beijing started to act like a world power.

The mega event's legacy

The days of Olympia are long gone and Beijing is again clouded by a milky-white haze. Five million cars frequent the streets of the capital today; during the Olympic Games there were 1.5 million. The sporting event was unable to change the government's principle of 'development trumps environmental protection' in the long run, says Lo Sze Ping, campaign manager at Greenpeace China. Due to the Games, today's city is at least much greener than it used to be. The new underground trains are always so packed that it is hard to imagine that the city was once able to do without them. The Olympic Green in the north of the city is a blessing for the smog-plagued city. The facilities complete with meadows, woods and water bodies are almost twice as large as Central Park in New York City. Beijing is thus home to the largest city park in the world and China has another superlative to call its own. The considerable construction and maintenance costs seem well-invested: thousands of citizens use the park to regenerate from stressful capital city life. The numerous office buildings that were built in the course of the Olympic construction frenzy are not as fully utilised. Many are vacant. But the challenge that trumps it all is the sensible utilisation of the gigantic sporting venues. The 31 stadiums cost 13 billion yuan (1.8 billion euros) and also today, long after the Games have come to a close, maintenance bills run up a huge tally.

6 — Chou Tao, team leader of the Chinese rhythmic gymnastics team in 2008, on the Olympic Park premises in Beijing.

7 — A souvenir photo in front of the National Stadium in Beijing is a must-have for many tourists.

das imposante, vielfach ausgezeichnete Nationalstadion, das liebevoll Vogelnest genannt wird. Ai Weiwei sagte trocken, dass er nicht
an der Einweihungszeremonie am 8. August 2008 teilnehmen würde –
wegen der politischen Umstände in China. «Keine Demokratie, keine
Bürgerrechte, ein Mangel an Gleichheit und Gerechtigkeit, nur Betrug
und Verrat», kritisierte der Künstler sein Heimatland. Er sei gegen
Olympische Spiele, in deren Namen die Menschenrechte verletzt
würden – zum Beispiel, indem Wanderarbeiter während der Spiele die
Stadt verlassen müssten. Die Spiele seien wie ein «falsches Lächeln»
für die Ausländer. Kultur werde für Propagandazwecke missbraucht.

Die Eröffnungszeremonie war spektakulär inszeniert. Eine gigantische Selbstdarstellung, mit der die Kommunistische Partei sich
vor der Welt in Szene setzte und ihren Machtanspruch gegenüber dem
eigenen Volk legitimieren wollte. Die Feier markierte den vorläu-
figen Höhepunkt einer eindrucksvollen Entwicklung, die 30 Jahre
zuvor mit der wirtschaftlichen Öffnung Chinas gegenüber dem Westen
begonnen hatte. 80 Staats- und Regierungschefs reisten nach Peking,
noch nie zuvor nahmen so viele Machthaber aus aller Welt an einer
olympischen Eröffnungsfeier teil. Einige Monate zuvor war noch von
Boykott die Rede gewesen, der Westen zeigte sich empört über die
Niederschlagung der Aufstände in Tibet im März 2008.

Als «Spiele der Superlative» gingen die Olympischen Sommerspiele
2008 in die Geschichte ein. Die olympische Idee aber, die auch den
Menschenrechten verpflichtet ist, wurde in Peking infrage gestellt.
Inhaftierte Regimekritiker, ausgebeutete Bauarbeiter, platt ge-
walzte Wohnviertel und die Medienzensur wurden vom Westen kritisiert.
Doch die Chinesen reagieren mittlerweile allergisch darauf, wenn
der Westen mit seinem universellen Anspruch zum Rundumschlag aus-
holt. Die Olympischen Spiele in Peking zeigten, dass China nicht
mehr gewillt ist, die Vormachtstellung des Westens einfach hinzu-

8 — Im Inneren des als «Vogelnest» bezeichneten
«Nationalstadions» wird für ein Musical geprobt.

Chou Tao, winner of an Olympic silver medal, reminisces about her
big moment surrounded by half-
empty stadiums: 'Standing on the
rostrum, everything was perfect.
But soon after the Games ended,
I somehow felt lost. My dream of so
many years had come true. Suddenly
I no longer knew what I was working towards, what I should do in
the future.' Her statement reflects
the general mood on the Olympic
grounds after the Games drew to a
close. In the summer of 2008, the
gigantic National Stadium designed
by the Swiss architect duo Herzog &
de Meuron was the centre of the
sporting world. Today, the Bird's
Nest is very rarely the venue of an
event. Here and there, paint is
cracking and a layer of dust coats
the steel construction. The Olympic Park attracts mainly tourists.
In the first year after the Games,
official sources recorded 20,000
visitors to the National Stadium,
eager to relive the Olympic spirit
one more time. 'We only saw the
stadium on TV, now I am here. It is
unbelievable. I am happy to be

here', a tourist from Hong Kong
says. A tourist group from South
China is also enthralled. At
six euros, the entry fee is rather
hefty, but it is practically a civic
duty to have one's picture taken
in the new landmark of the capital.

Building the National Stadium
cost 3.5 billion yuan (492 million
euros). The operators hope that the
annual maintenance costs of about
ten million euros will be matched
by the entry fees, because sporting
events alone will never be able to
cover the costs. Negotiations with
local football clubs ended without results. So far, some concerts
have taken place in the arena and
the 60th birthday of the Communist
Party was celebrated with a new
staging of the Puccini opera *Turandot*. There are motor shows and
artificial winter landscapes. The
greatest sporting event since
the 2008 Summer Games were the 15th
World Championships in Athletics
in August 2015. Beijing won the
bid after London withdrew its
application, leaving the Chinese
capital the sole contender.

The administration of the Olympic
Park exudes optimism, claiming
that the Bird's Nest, the swimming
stadium and the fencing centre
are booked to capacity. And the
sporting venues in the Olympic
Park reportedly generate profits,
even though hardly any sporting
events take place there anymore.

The operators had high hopes
for the national swimming stadium
after the Games. The building
clad in a honeycomb of changing
colours, affectionately dubbed
Water Cube, was reopened as Asia's
largest water park, offering
water slides, a wave pool and a
stage for shows. The refurbishment
is rumoured to have amounted
to 200 million yuan (23 million
euros); the original construction
budget was 1.1 billion yuan (154
million euros). A corner of the
stadium was maintained for competitions. The 177-metre swimming
pool has hosted a number of water
ballets and shows. The original
seating capacity of 17,000 was reduced to 6,000. Chinese tourists
are fascinated by the pool in

nehmen. China war daran, sich zu modernisieren und Peking fing an, sich wie eine Weltmacht zu benehmen.

Das Erbe der Mega-Party

Die Tage von Olympia sind längst vorbei und über Peking hängt wieder ein milchiger Dunst. Heute fahren fünf Millionen Autos auf den Straßen der Hauptstadt, während der Spiele waren es 1,5 Millionen. Ein Sportanlass konnte den Regierungsgrundsatz «Entwicklung vor Umweltschutz» langfristig nicht ändern, sagt Lo Sze Ping, Kampagnenmanager bei Greenpeace China. Dank den Spielen ist die Stadt heute zumindest viel grüner. Auch sind die neuen U-Bahn-Züge stets so voll, dass es unmöglich erscheint, dass die Stadt je ohne sie auskommen konnte. Ein Segen für die smoggeplagte Stadt ist der olympische Park nördlich des Sportgeländes. Die Anlage mit Wiesen, Wäldern und Gewässern ist fast doppelt so groß wie der Central Park in New York. Peking hat somit den größten Stadtpark der Welt und China ist um einen Superlativ reicher. Die beachtlichen Bau- und Unterhaltskosten scheinen sich zu lohnen: Tausende Bürger entspannen sich hier von den Strapazen der Hauptstadt. Weniger ausgelastet sind die vielen Bürohochhäuser, die im olympischen Bauboom aus dem Boden schossen. Viele stehen leer. Die größte Herausforderung jedoch ist die sinnvolle Nutzung der riesigen Sportstätten. Die 31 Stadien haben 13 Milliarden Yuan (1,8 Milliarden Euro) gekostet — und verschlingen auch nach den Spielen eine ganze Menge Cash. Chou Tao, die Olympia-Silbermedaillengewinnerin, steht auf dem Gelände zwischen den halbleeren Stadien und denkt noch einmal an ihren großen Moment: «Als ich auf dem Podest stand, war alles perfekt. Aber dann, nach den Wettkämpfen, fühlte ich mich irgendwie verloren. Nach so vielen Jahren ist mein Traum wahr geworden. Plötz-

9 — Der neue Park «Olympic Green» ist mit einer Fläche von über 800 Hektar einer der größten Stadtparks der Welt.

which Michael Phelps swam Olympic history: 'It feels good to be here. The children can swim here and imagine what Michael Phelps felt like when he won eight gold medals.' To make such dreams come true, the training pool was opened to the tourist masses as well. Visitors pay 100 yuan (14 euros) to play and swim here, patriotic shudders included.

White elephants and pink glasses

The former fencing hall offers 270,000 square metres to interested parties who wish to host new large-scale events. Renovating the entire building took over a year. Where contestants fenced over Olympic gold medals during the Games, today international conferences, company events, exhibitions and shows are held. The fencing centre's manager is reluctant to talk about revenues, but stresses that the project is in line with the budget plan. 'We want to become the best conven-

tion centre in Asia. There is real money to be made in the conference business', said CEO Liu Haiying shortly after the renovation.

It's every Olympic city's challenge to save the stadiums from turning into white elephants. In Beijing, some post-Olympic utilisations work better than others: the smaller halls on the university grounds are used by students and most apartments in the Olympic Village have been sold. The gigantic stadiums, however, are reminders of the questionable legacy of the mega event, which was staged to extravagantly celebrate the state without consideration for costs or environmental protection.

The former Shunyi Olympic Rowing-Canoeing Park, the largest venue of the Summer Games in terms of surface area, is a sad sight today. Canoeing, rowing and long-distance-swimming competitors once made for the finishing line watched by 25,000 visitors. Today, the water sports park lies abandoned. The same holds true for the Olympic remnants in the

8 — Rehearsals for a musical inside the National Stadium, also known as the Bird's Nest.

9 — At over 800 hectares, the new Olympic Green is among the world's largest city parks.

lich wusste ich nicht mehr, was mein Ziel war, was ich in Zukunft machen soll.» Ihre Aussage steht stellvertretend für die Stimmung auf dem Olympiagelände post festum. Das gigantische Nationalstadion der Schweizer Architekten Herzog & de Meuron war im Sommer 2008 der Mittelpunkt der Sportwelt. Heute wird das Vogelnest kaum noch für Anlässe genutzt. Hier und dort blättert etwas Lack ab und auf dem Stahlgerüst lagert eine Schicht Staub. Das olympische Gelände ist vor allem eine Touristenattraktion. Im ersten Jahr nach den Spielen strömten laut offiziellen Angaben noch 20 000 Besucher in das Stadion, um den olympischen Geist nochmals zu erleben. «Wir haben das Stadion nur im Fernsehen gesehen, jetzt bin ich hier. Es ist unglaublich. Ich bin glücklich, hier zu sein», sagt ein Tourist aus Hongkong. Auch eine Touristengruppe aus Südchina ist entzückt. Mit sechs Euro ist der Eintrittspreis ziemlich hoch, doch es gehört quasi zur Bürgerpflicht, sich in dem neuen Wahrzeichen der Hauptstadt ablichten zu lassen.

3,5 Milliarden Yuan (492 Millionen Euro) betrugen die Baukosten des Nationalstadions. Die Betreiber hoffen, dass sie den Unterhalt von rund zehn Millionen Euro pro Jahr unter anderem über Eintrittspreise wettmachen können, denn Sportveranstaltungen werden nicht ausreichen, um die Kosten zu decken. Die Verhandlungen mit lokalen Fußballclubs haben sich zerschlagen. In der Arena fanden einige Konzerte statt, zum 60. Geburtstag der Kommunistischen Partei wurde die Puccini-Oper «Turandot» neu inszeniert. Es gibt Autoshows und künstliche Winterlandschaften. Der größte Sportanlass seit den Sommerspielen 2008 waren die 15. Leichtathletik-Weltmeisterschaften im August 2015. Peking erhielt den Zuschlag, nachdem London seine Bewerbung zurückgezogen hatte und die chinesische Hauptstadt einziger Bewerber war.

10 — Im Velodrom «Laoshan» sind auch die Trainingshallen der Fechter untergebracht.

11 — Das Velodrom ist menschenleer und im Alltag nur mit Tageslicht erhellt, wird aber immer noch für Radrennen und als Trainingszentrum genutzt.

city quarter Wukesong in the west of Beijing. The baseball stadium was torn down and the basketball hall stands mostly unused. Following the Olympic Games, the building with a seating capacity of 18,000 that cost 1.4 billion yuan (197 million euros) was vacant for more than a year. Today, it hosts some basketball games every year, such as the games of the Beijing basketball club.

The government of the People's Republic has rented out the stadiums to operator companies, but retains a majority stake or is at least the co-owner of the halls in most cases. It is probably due to the government's efforts that Beijing's Olympic venues will continue to be open to the public in the future, at least as a tourist attraction. The distinctive stadiums in Beijing stand for much more than two glorious sporting weeks in the summer of 2008. The government seemed set to stage the Olympic Games as the seal on China's rise to becoming a modern world power.

10 — The Laoshan velodrome also houses training halls for fencing.

11 — The deserted velodrome is only lit by daylight during the day, but it is still used for cycling races and as a training centre.

Die Verwaltung des Olympiaparks gibt sich zuversichtlich: Das Vogelnest, die Schwimmhalle und das Fechtzentrum seien gut ausgelastet. Die Sportstätten im Olympiapark erwirtschaften Gewinne, heißt es, auch wenn hier kaum mehr Sportanlässe stattfinden.

Für das nationale Schwimmstadion versprachen sich die Betreiber nach den Spielen großen Erfolg. Das Gebäude mit der farblich wechselnden Wabenfassade – liebevoll Wasserwürfel genannt – wurde als Asiens größter Wasserpark wiedereröffnet, mit Rutschbahnen, Wellenbad und einer Bühne für Aufführungen. Die Renovierung soll 200 Millionen Yuan (23 Millionen Euro) gekostet haben, das ursprüngliche Baubudget betrug 1,1 Milliarden Yuan (154 Millionen Euro). Eine Ecke blieb für Wettkämpfe erhalten. Im 177 Meter langen Schwimmbecken fanden einige Wasserballetts und Shows statt. Die 17 000 Zuschauerplätze wurden auf 6000 reduziert. Die chinesischen Touristen sind beeindruckt vom Anblick des Beckens, in dem Michael Phelps Olympiageschichte schwamm: «Es fühlt sich gut an, hier zu sein. Die Kinder können hier schwimmen und dabei spüren, wie Michael Phelps acht Goldmedaillen gewann.» Damit solche Träume wahr werden, wurde auch der Trainingspool für die Touristenmassen geöffnet. 100 Yuan (14 Euro) bezahlt man, um hier zu plantschen und zu schwimmen, patriotischer Schauer inbegriffen.

Weisse Elefanten und eine rosarote Brille

Die ehemalige Fechthalle bietet auf 270 000 Quadratmetern Platz für neue Großprojekte. Über ein Jahr dauerte der Umbau des ganzen Gebäudes. Wo während der Olympischen Spiele um Gold gefochten wurde, finden jetzt internationale Konferenzen, Firmenanlässe, Ausstellungen und Aufführungen jeglicher Art statt. Der Manager der Fechthalle will nicht über Umsätze sprechen, versichert aber, dass man im Budgetplan liege. «Wir wollen das beste Konferenzzentrum Asiens werden. Mit dem Konferenzbusiness lässt sich Geld verdienen», sagt der Vorstandsvorsitzende Liu Haiying kurz nach dem Umbau.

Es ist die Herausforderung jeder Olympiastadt, die Stadien nicht zu weißen Elefanten verkommen zu lassen. In Peking funktionieren einige Nachnutzungen besser als andere: Die kleineren Hallen auf den Universitätsgeländen werden von den Studenten genutzt und die meisten Wohnungen im Olympiadorf wurden verkauft. Die imposanten Stadien jedoch erinnern an das eher zweifelhafte Erbe der Mega-Party, die ohne Rücksichtnahme auf Kostenfragen und Umweltschutz als gigantische Selbstfeier inszeniert wurde.

Der ehemalige Ruder- und Kanupark, die flächenmäßig größte Anlage der Sommerspiele, bietet ein trostloses Bild. Kanuten, Ruderer und Langstreckenschwimmer gingen hier vor 25 000 Zuschauern an den Start, heute liegt der Wassersportpark brach. Auch die olympischen Hinterlassenschaften im Westpekinger Stadtviertel Wukesong sind nicht gut ausgelastet. Das Baseballstadion wurde abgerissen und die Basketballhalle steht oft leer. Nach den Olympischen Spielen stand der 1,4 Milliarden Yuan (197 Millionen Euro) teure Bau mit seinen 18 000 Sitzplätzen über ein Jahr lang leer. Heute finden einige Basketballspiele im Jahr statt, wie zum Beispiel die Spiele des Pekinger Basketballclubs.

Der Staat hat die Stadien an Betreiberfirmen vermietet, besitzt jedoch in den meisten Fällen die Mehrheit oder ist zumindest Miteigentümer der Hallen. Die Regierung dürfte dafür sorgen, dass Pekings Olympiastätten weiter geöffnet bleiben, zumindest als Touristenattraktionen. Die markanten Stadien in Peking verkörpern viel mehr als zwei glorreiche Sportwochen im Sommer 2008. Die Regierung schien die Olympischen Spiele als Besiegelung für Chinas Aufstieg zur modernen Weltmacht zu inszenieren.

Barbara Lüthi, geboren 1973, begann ihre Laufbahn als Journalistin nach einem Sprachaufenthalt in Sydney mit einer eigenen Talkshow beim Privatsender Star TV. Ab 2001 arbeitete die Zürcherin für das Polit- und Wirtschaftsmagazin Rundschau. Für ihre Reportage über die Arbeitsbedingungen in den chinesischen Spielzeugfabriken gewann Lüthi 2005 den «CNN Journalist Award». Von 2006 bis Anfang 2014 war sie Chinakorrespondentin des Schweizer Radio- und Fernsehsenders SRF und wurde von CNN 2008 für eine Reportage über chinesische Landenteignungen als «Journalistin des Jahres» im deutschsprachigen Raum ausgezeichnet. 2014 erschien Lüthis erstes Buch «Live aus China», das die Sachbuch-Bestsellerliste erreichte. Barbara Lüthi lebt mit ihren zwei Kindern in Hongkong.

Following a language stay in Sydney, Barbara Lüthi, born in 1973, started her career as a journalist with her own talk show at the private television station Star TV. From 2001, Lüthi, who is originally from Zurich, Switzerland, worked for the Swiss politics and business news show *Rundschau*. In 2005, Lüthi was awarded the 'CNN Journalist Award' for her report on the labour conditions in Chinese toy factories. From 2006 to early 2014, she was China correspondent for the Swiss radio and TV broadcaster SRF. In 2008, CNN named her 'Journalist of the Year' in the German-speaking region for a report on land confiscation in China. In 2014, Lüthi's first book, *Live aus China* (Live from China), was published and climbed the bestseller lists for non-fiction. Barbara Lüthi lives in Hong Kong with her two children.

Fahrunterricht vor dem Velodrom im Pekinger Distrikt Shijingshan
Driving lessons in front of the velodrome in the Shijingshan district in Beijing

Außenhülle des Velodroms «Laoshan»
Exterior of the Laoshan velodrome

Wachmann am Eingang zum Velodrom
Security guard at the entrance to the velodrome

Überreste der olympischen Mountainbike-Rennstrecke
The remains of the Olympic Mountain Bike Course

Ungenutzte Plakatwand an der Mountainbike-Rennstrecke
Unused billboard on the Mountain Bike Course

Von einem Zirkus genutzte Brachfläche neben dem Olympiapark
The fallow area next to the Olympic Park is the temporary home to a circus

Shaolin-Schüler warten auf ihren Einsatz bei Proben im «Nationalstadion»
Shaolin students waiting for their turn during rehearsals at the National Stadium

Viele Chinesen sind stolz auf ihr «Nationalstadion»
Many Chinese are proud of their National Stadium

Parkfeld vor dem nationalen Schwimmstadion «Aquatics Center»
Parking area in front of the Aquatics Center, the national swimming stadium

Schwimmstadion «Aquatics Center»
The Aquatics Center swimming stadium

Ungenutztes Stadion der Ruderanlage «Shunyi» im Nordosten von Peking
A deserted stadium at the Shunyi rowing facilities in the northeast of Beijing

Wachmann beim künstlich angelegten See der Ruderanlage
A guard at the artificial lake of the rowing facilities

Wildwasseranlage «Shunyi»
The whitewater slalom course at Shunyi

Eigentumswohnungen im Olympischen Dorf
Owner-occupied houses in the Olympic Village

Abendstimmung im Olympiapark
Twilight at the Olympic Park

«Nationalstadion»
The National Stadium

SOTSCHI 2014
OLYMPISCHE WINTERSPIELE

Das staubige Herz der größten
Baustelle der Welt

Essay von Martin Müller

SOCHI 2014
WINTER OLYMPICS

The Dusty Heart of the World's
Largest Construction Site

Essay by Martin Müller

1 — Busterminal beim Olympiapark in Sotschi-Adler.

2 – Das Neubaugebiet «Nekrasovskoe» wurde für Bewohner gebaut, die dem Olympiapark weichen mussten.

3 – Die Rentnerin Ekaterina kennt das Quartier noch aus der Zeit vor der touristischen Hochblüte in den 1970er- und 1980er-Jahren.

4 – Eine der vielen Neubausiedlungen nahe des Olympiaparks.

5 – Ein Spielplatz im Quartier «Nekrasovskoe», dem Umsiedlungs- und Vorzeigeprojekt der Regierung.

Man merkt Julia Erofeeva am Lächeln an, dass sie über 63 Jahre irgendwann gelernt hat, den Gang der Dinge hinzunehmen. Wir stehen auf der Anhöhe gleich hinter der Imeretinskaja-Bucht bei der Ortschaft Adler, 30 Kilometer südlich von Sotschi, und blicken auf das Schwarze Meer. Für das schattige Plätzchen unter den Kiefern bin ich dankbar, denn der Sommer in diesem Jahr, 2011, legt sich ins Zeug. Der heiße Wind lässt keine Zweifel aufkommen: Sotschi, die Sommerhauptstadt Russlands, liegt tatsächlich auf demselben Breitengrad wie die Côte d'Azur.

Von dem kleinen Hügel öffnet sich ein weiter Blick. Hinter uns liegt die Vergangenheit: ein kleiner orthodoxer Friedhof, viele Gräber bereits überwuchert, viele Menschen seit mehreren Jahrzehnten tot. An den Gräbern zeugen Zeichen vergangener Zeiten von einst stolzen Leben: Heldin der Arbeit, verdienter Künstler der UdSSR, Veteran in Afghanistan. Vor uns hingegen liegt die Zukunft. Dort unten in der Bucht schlägt im stumpfen Gleichtakt der 40-Tonner das staubige Herz der größten Baustelle der Welt: der olympische Park, die Drehscheibe der Olympischen Winterspiele 2014. Sechs Stadien, gruppiert um eine leere Mitte. Durch die vor Hitze wabernde Luft erscheinen sie fast wie ein Phantasma – eigentlich wie die gesamte Idee: Winterspiele in den Subtropen.

Es sind bisher nur Gerippe, die mit den gerenderten Hochglanzbildern der 3D-Visualisierungen wenig gemein haben. Staub wirbelt auf, wo Lastwagen im Minutentakt Aushub weg- und Baumaterial herankarren. Dort, wo im Februar 2014 Athleten die Medaillen umgehängt wurden, stand bis vor kurzem Julia Erofeevas Häuschen. Zusammen mit 800 anderen Bewohnern musste sie dem olympischen Park Platz machen. Nun wohnt sie in einem Haus im neu angelegten Dorf Nekrasovskoe: zwar ohne ihren Gemüsegarten, aber dafür in einem Vorstadtidyll, das in seiner Aufgeräumtheit geradewegs dem amerikanischen Traum entsprungen zu sein scheint.

Sotschi – Stadt von Gottes Gnaden

«Gott erschuf Sotschi; der Teufel Mogotschi», so lautet eine Volksweisheit, die Bewohner Sotschis gerne zitieren. In der Tat, wer von Mogotschi an der transsibirischen Eisenbahn im Fernen Osten Russlands nach Sotschi reist – und die sechs Tage im stickigen Zugabteil hinter sich gebracht hat –, dem mag Sotschi wie der Himmel auf Erden erscheinen. Auf 44 Grad nördlicher Breite gelegen, befindet sich die Stadt auf ähnlicher geographischer Breite wie Nizza oder Genua. Bei einer jährlichen Durchschnittstemperatur von mehr als 13 Grad Celsius übertrifft Sotschi die Werte von Vancouver, dem bisher klimatisch wärmsten Ort der Winterspiele im Jahr 2010, um stattliche 3 Grad Celsius. Palmen, Eukalypten und Oleander

Yulia Erofeeva's faint smile reveals that she has learned to accept the course of things over the past 63 years. We are standing on a hill, just behind the Imeretinskaya Bay, near the district of Adler, 30 kilometres south of Sochi, and looking out into the Black Sea. I am grateful for the little shade provided by the pine trees, because the summer this year, 2011, is intense. The hot wind leaves no doubt that Sochi, Russia's summer capital, is actually located on the same latitude as the Côte d'Azur.

From the little hill, a sweeping vista opens up before our eyes. Behind us lies the past: a small orthodox cemetery with many graves overgrown, many of the people resting here have been dead for decades. Some tomb stones are a testament to formerly proud lives: heroine of labour, distinguished artist of the USSR, Afghanistan veteran. And before us lies the future: down in the bay, in dull common mode, the excavators work the dusty heart of the world's largest construction site: the Olympic Park, the hub of the 2014 Olympic Winter Games. Six stadiums, arranged around an empty centre. Through the billowing heat, they almost seem like a phantasm – so does the very notion: Winter Games in a subtropical region.

So far, we can only see skeletons that have little resemblance to the rendered glossy pictures of the 3D visualisations. Dust whirls up where 40-ton trucks cart off excavated soil and deliver construction materials at minute intervals. The site where in February 2014 athletes would receive their winning medals is also the place where Yulia Erofeeva's little house used to stand – but that, too, is a thing of the past. Together with 800 other people, she had to make space for the Olympic Park. Now she lives in a house in the newly designed village of Nekrasovskoe. She no longer has her vegetable garden, but instead lives in a suburban idyll that is so neat and uniform it looks like the American dream come true.

Sochi – a city by the grace of God

The people of Sochi like to say: 'God created Sochi, the devil created Mogochi.' Indeed, to those who travel from Mogochi in the far east of Russia to Sochi with the Trans-Siberian Railway – that is to those who spend six days in a badly ventilated train compartment – Sochi might appear like heaven on earth. The city lies at 44 degrees northern latitude, comparable to the latitude of Nice or Genoa. With an annual average temperature of 13 degrees Celsius, Sochi is warmer than Vancouver, which had held the record of the hottest venue of Olympic Winter Games since 2010, by three degrees Celsius. Palm and eucalyptus trees and oleander are signs of the subtropical climate and lend the region a southern flair. Sochi is not considered the heart of the Russian riviera on the Black Sea coast for nothing. The agglomeration spans 140 kilometres of coast all the way to the border with

zeigen das subtropische Klima an und verleihen der Region ein südländisches Gepräge. Nicht umsonst gilt Sotschi als das Herzstück der russischen Riviera an der Schwarzmeerküste. Die Agglomeration erstreckt sich über mehr als 140 Kilometer entlang der Küste bis hin zur Grenze mit Abchasien, der abtrünnigen Republik Georgiens, und umfasst knapp eine halbe Million Einwohner. In der Kernstadt selbst wohnen allerdings nur gut 150 000 Personen. Sotschi ist mehr ein Siedlungsband denn eine klar definierte Stadt.

Traditionell gilt Sotschi als Sommerhauptstadt *(Letnjaja Stolitsa)* Russlands und hat sich insbesondere auf den Badetourismus spezialisiert. In der Sowjetunion galt Sotschi als der wohl mondänste Erholungsort und war gleichzeitig Modellstadt für den sowjetischen Tourismus. Viele Gewerkschaften unterhielten dort prestigeträchtige Sanatorien; einige davon kann man heute noch in ihrer alten Pracht bewundern. Eine Reise *(putëvka)* nach Sotschi galt als Privileg und war neben der Nomenklatura hauptsächlich verdienten Arbeiterinnen und Arbeitern vorbehalten. Während des zehnten Fünfjahresplans von 1976 bis 1980 kamen insgesamt 47 Millionen Erholungssuchende in dieses wahrhaft göttliche Paradies.

Doch mit dem Zusammenbruch der Sowjetunion 1991 ging es mit dem Tourismus bergab. In den 1990er-Jahren hatten die russischen Bürger schlichtweg andere Sorgen als in den Urlaub zu fahren; es ging ums nackte Überleben. Mit dem wirtschaftlichen Aufschwung seit Anfang der 2000er-Jahre bevorzugen russische Bürger zunehmend Destinationen jenseits des vormaligen Eisernen Vorhangs für den Sommerurlaub, statt in die als überteuert und überholt geltenden Zentren des Sowjettourismus von einst zurückzukehren.

Mehr als 20 Jahre nach dem Zusammenbruch der Sowjetunion kommen weit weniger Gäste an die russische Riviera als noch während der Blütezeiten der Sowjetunion. Wie viel weniger genau, das weiß keiner so richtig. Der Bürgermeister Sotschis, Anatoli Pachomow, sprach in einem Jahr von vier Millionen Gästeankünften in der Sommersaison, dann jedoch nur noch von drei. Realistischer erscheint die Zahl von ein bis eineinhalb Millionen Gästen über das gesamte Jahr. Zudem ist die Aufenthaltsdauer zurückgegangen: Blieben Gäste früher im Durchschnitt neun Tage, so sind es jetzt gerade einmal fünf. Die Unternehmer in Sotschi spüren seit 2014 auch die Konkurrenz durch die Krim, die mit günstigeren Preisen lockt und wo man als spendabler Urlauber gleichzeitig auch noch seiner patriotischen Verpflichtung zum Aufbau des neuen Landesteils nachkommen kann. Kurzum: Der Tourismusbetrieb in Sotschi ist nur noch ein Abglanz vergangener Größe. Für eine dringend benötigte Frischzellenkur kamen die Olympischen Winterspiele da gerade recht.

Abkhazia, a break-away republic of Georgia, and has a population of close to 500,000 people. The urban core, however, is home to just about 150,000 people. Sochi is not a clearly defined city but rather resembles a belt settlement.

Traditionally, Sochi has been viewed as the summer capital of Russia, the *Letnyaya Stolitsa,* and has specialised in seaside tourism. Back in the days of the Soviet Union, Sochi was considered by far the most glamorous health resort and also served as a model city for Soviet tourism. Many unions had prestigious sanatoriums there, some of them still maintain their former splendour and accept visitors. A journey, or *putëvka,* to Sochi was seen as a privilege and was, apart from the Russian elite, primarily reserved for merited workers. During the Tenth Five-Year Plan from 1976 to 1980, a total of 47 million holiday makers visited this truly divine paradise.

Tourism declined, however, in the aftermath of the collapse of the Soviet Union. In the 1990s, the Russian people simply had other things to worry about than going on vacation; they struggled with bare survival. Since the economic upswing of the early 2000s, Russians have started to prefer destinations outside the former Iron Curtain for summer vacations instead of returning to the former centres of Soviet tourism that they often consider overpriced and outdated.

Today, more than 20 years after the collapse of the Soviet Union, far fewer people find their way to the Russian riviera than during its Soviet heyday. But no one knows exactly how much the numbers have dropped. Sochi's mayor, Anatoliy Pakhomov, reported four million visitors for the summer season one year, at another occasion he spoke of only three million. Between one and one and a half million guests over the period of a year is a more realistic estimate. The stays have also become shorter. While guests used to stay for an average of nine days, they now stay for only five.

Since 2014, entrepreneurs in Sochi have also had to fight an unexpected competitor: Crimea. Now part of the Russian Federation, the peninsula not only lures Russians with lower prices but also gives generous holiday makers a chance to meet their patriotic obligation to contribute to the development of a new region. In a nutshell: tourism in Sochi is only a pale reflection of its former glory. The Olympic Winter Games came just in time for a much-needed rejuvenation.

A fantasy of dirt and steel

The vision for the winter sports makeover of Sochi was nothing less than grandiose. Established resorts of the international winter jet set, from Aspen, Colorado, to St. Moritz and Zermatt in Switzerland, served as the benchmarks for the new Sochi. Vladimir Putin had big plans. Sochi is the Olympic fantasy of a modern czar, cast in dirt and steel.

6 — Winterolympiade am sonnigen Strand
bei 18 Grad Celsius.

7 — Fernsehübertragungswagen im Skigebiet
«Rosa Khutor».

8 – Russische Nachwuchssportler besuchen den
Olympiapark in Sotschi-Adler.

9 – Volunteers versammeln sich vor dem Eisstadion
«Bolschoi».

10 – Die Olympischen Spiele sind vor allem auch
ein Medienereignis. Eines von vielen mobilen
Fernsehstudios auf dem Gelände des Olympiaparks. Das Moskauer Polizeiorchester singt im
amerikanischen Fernsehen.

11 – Die riesige, provisorische Zuschauertribüne im
Zielgelände der alpinen Skiwettbewerbe.

Fantasie aus Erde und Stahl

Die Vision für das wintersportliche Makeover Sotschis war dabei nichts weniger als göttlich. Die Messlatte für das neue Sotschi sollten die arrivierten Ressorts des globalen Wintersport-Jetsets bilden – von Aspen über St. Moritz bis Zermatt. Dafür hatte Putin groß angerichtet. Sotschi ist die Erde und Stahl gewordene Fantasie von Olympia eines modernen Zaren.

Die Winterspiele reihen sich in eine ganze Serie an Großprojekten in Russland ein, die bis ins 18. Jahrhundert zurückreicht, als Peter der Große die Sümpfe am Finnischen Meerbusen trockenlegen liess, um St. Petersburg und seine Residenz Peterhof zu bauen. Zar Alexander III. nahm den Bau der transsibirischen Eisenbahn auf, welche Leonid Breschnew in den 1970er-Jahren durch die Baikal-Amur-Magistrale ergänzte. Lenin wollte den Kommunismus unter anderem mittels «Elektrifizierung des ganzen Landes» verwirklichen – ein Anliegen, das er zur Staatsdoktrin erhob. In der Regierungszeit Stalins wurde das hochmoderne Stahlkombinat Magnitogorsk aus dem Boden gestampft, das eine konkrete Manifestation der kommunistischen Sozialutopie darstellen sollte.

Die russischen Großprojekte sind deshalb so interessant, weil sie ein Spiegel der Hoffnungen, Sehnsüchte und des Selbstverständnisses des Landes, seiner Bewohner und seiner Herrscher sind. Das gilt auch für Sotschi und die Winterspiele. Sie sind wie ein Mikrokosmos des heutigen Russlands. Auf engstem Raum spielt sich dort das ab, was im Land selbst in viel größerem Stil abläuft: die Suche nach Anerkennung auf der Weltbühne, die Konzentration von Ressourcen in den Händen weniger, der Wandel zur hedonistischen Freizeitgesellschaft und der Vorrang der Staatsräson gegenüber den Interessen der einzelnen Bürgerinnen und Bürger.

Die Olympischen Spiele in Sotschi sollten ein russisches St. Moritz kreieren und gleichzeitig Russlands Ruf als touristische Destination aufpolieren. Russland, so die gängige Devise, habe viel mehr zu bieten als militärische Stärke und Öl und Gas. Putin sah die Verleihung der Austragungsrechte daher «nicht nur als Anerkennung der Errungenschaften Russlands im Sport, sondern als Urteil über unser Land und seine wachsenden Möglichkeiten». Ganz ähnlich schrieb die Tageszeitung Wedomosti, dass der Sieg Sotschis über die Mitbewerber in Österreich und Südkorea von der Bevölkerung und der politischen Elite des Landes als Symbol der wiedergewonnenen Stärke Russlands wahrgenommen werde. Die Olympischen Spiele – sie sind Putins nationale Idee.

Nach Moskau und St. Petersburg soll Sotschi zur dritten Stadt Russlands werden. Während

The Olympic Winter Games are part of a whole series of large-scale projects in Russia that go all the way back to the 18th century when Peter the Great ordered the drainage of the swamps in the Gulf of Finland to build St. Petersburg and his residence Peterhof Palace. Czar Alexander III initiated the Trans-Siberian Railway project, which Leonid Brezhnev extended in the 1970s with the Baikal-Amur Magistral railway. Lenin wanted to implement communism by 'electrifying the entire country' – a matter which he turned into a state doctrine. Stalin set up the state-of-the-art Magnitogorsk Iron and Steel Works and the city around it by decree. They were to represent a concrete manifestation of the communist social utopia.

Major Russian projects are so intriguing because they are a reflection of the hopes, aspirations and the self-image of the country, its people and its rulers. This also applies to Sochi and the Winter Games. They represent a microcosm of today's Russia.

The goings-on in this small area show what is happening in the entire country on a much larger scale: the search for international recognition, a handful of people controlling most of the resources, a trend towards a hedonistic leisure society and the privilege of the raison d'État over the interest of the individual citizen.

The Olympic Games in Sochi were to create the Russian version of St. Moritz and simultaneously spruce up Russia's reputation as a tourist destination. It is commonplace in Russia to say that the country has much more to offer than military strength, oil and gas. Vladimir Putin thus considered winning the rights to hold the event 'not only a recognition of Russia's accomplishments in sports, but also a verdict on our country and its growing opportunities.' The daily newspaper *Vedomosti* similarly wrote that the people and the political elite of the country saw the victory of Sochi over Austria and South

1 – Bus terminal at the Olympic Park in Adler, Sochi.

2 – The new residential area Nekrasovskoe houses people whose homes had to make way for the Olympic Park.

3 – Retired Ekaterina has known the district even before it became a tourist hotspot in the 1970s and 1980s.

4 – One of the many new housing quarters close to the Olympic Park.

5 – A playground in Nekrasovskoe, the government's showcase resettlement project.

6 – Winter Olympics at the beach, at sunshine and 18 degrees Celsius.

7 – Broadcast vans in the Rosa Khutor ski resort.

8 – Young Russian athletes visit the Olympic Park in Adler, Sochi.

9 – Volunteers gather in front of the Bolshoy Ice Dome.

10 – The Olympic Games are above all a media event. One of many mobile broadcasting stations on the Olympic Park's premises. The Moscow Police Orchestra sings for a US-American TV station.

11 – The gigantic makeshift grandstands in the finish area for the alpine skiing competitions.

Moskau die Schaltzentrale politischer und wirtschaftlicher Macht darstellt und St. Petersburg die kulturelle Hauptstadt Russlands bildet, richtet das neue Sotschi sein Antlitz gen Westen: Lässig und entspannt lädt es die globale Freizeitgesellschaft ein, das Russland jenseits von Öl, Gas und Korruption kennenzulernen. Der Wahlspruch der Winterspiele in Sotschi, «Hot. Cool. Yours.» *(Žarkie. Zimnie. Tvoi.),* zielt auf den individualisierten Hedonisten ab, appelliert jedoch doppeldeutig auch an die Libido. Für Putin war unbestritten: «Sochi is going to become a new world class resort for the new Russia. And the whole world!»

Von Gewinnern und Verlierern
_____

Putins Vision hatte tiefgreifende Konsequenzen für die Region. Als Sotschi am 5. Juli 2007 die Winterspiele 2014 zugesprochen bekam, existierte nicht eine einzige olympiafähige Austragungsstätte. Im Kaukasusgebirge bei Sotschi gab es nur eine Handvoll alter Schlepp- und Sessellifte und es fehlten mehrere Zehntausend nach internationalem Standard klassifizierte Hotelzimmer. Die Region litt unter regelmäßigen Verkehrsinfarkten, sodass man im Auto für die 30 Kilometer vom Flughafen bis in die Stadt zur Hauptverkehrszeit teilweise mehr als zwei Stunden benötigte. Sotschi verbrauchte mehr Strom als es produzierte

und die überlasteten Netze brachen regelmäßig zusammen.

Zwölf Milliarden US-Dollar waren für die Vorbereitung auf die Winterspiele veranschlagt, aber schnell stellte sich heraus, dass diese Summe nicht annähernd ausreichen würde. Anfang 2013 veröffentlichte die Regierung eine neue Kostenschätzung von gut 50 Milliarden US-Dollar. Damit übertrifft die 16-tägige Großveranstaltung in Sotschi die bisher teuersten (und deutlich größeren!) Olympischen Sommerspiele in Peking 2008 um mehr als zehn Milliarden US-Dollar. Auch ein Jahr nach den Spielen sind die wahren Gesamtkosten noch nicht bekannt und es ist gut möglich, dass sie niemals veröffentlicht werden: Sie dürften noch um einiges über diesen Schätzungen liegen. Sotschi 2014 stellt somit ein extremes Beispiel von Regionalpolitik dar: Pro Einwohner Sotschis flossen circa 115 000 US-Dollar in die Region. Jede Russin und jeder Russe verzichtete damit implizit im Durchschnitt auf knapp 350 US-Dollar an staatlichen Mitteln.

Angesichts dieses Geldsegens müssten sich die Bewohner Sotschis glücklich schätzen, würde man meinen. Neue Straßen, zusätzliche Eisenbahnverbindungen, ein moderner Flughafen, eine zuverlässigere Stromversorgung, neue Arbeitsstellen, der Ausbau von touristischen Angeboten — was wünscht man sich mehr? Doch ist allerorts auch Frustration und Enttäuschung zu vernehmen.

Korea as a symbol of Russia's reclaimed power. The Olympic Games are Putin's national idea.

Following Moscow and St. Petersburg, Sochi was to become the third Russian city. While Moscow represents the political and economic hub and St. Petersburg the cultural centre of Russia, the new Sochi is supposed to look towards the West. In a casual and relaxed manner, it invites the international leisure society to get to know Russia beyond oil, gas and corruption. The slogan for the Winter Games in Sochi, 'Hot. Cool. Yours.' *(Žarkie. Zimnie. Tvoi.),* is directed at the individual hedonists, but also ambiguously appeals to their libido. For Putin there was no room for doubt: 'Sochi is going to become a new world-class resort for the new Russia. And the whole world!'

Of winners and losers
_____

Putin's vision had far-reaching consequences for the region. When Sochi won the right to host

the 2014 Winter Games on 5 July 2007, not a single Olympic venue existed. The Caucasus area near Sochi only had a handful of old T-bar and chair lifts and it lacked several tens of thousands of hotel rooms classified according to international standards. The region was regularly suffering from traffic congestions, at times turning the 30-kilometre trip from the airport to the city into a good two-hour drive during rush hour. Sochi consumed more electricity than it produced and the overloaded grids broke down time and again.

Twelve billion US dollars were projected for the preparations for the Winter Games, but it soon turned out that this amount would not nearly suffice. In early 2013, the government published a new cost estimate of around 50 billion US dollars. The investment for this mega event in Sochi thus trumped the most expensive (and noticeably bigger!) Olympic Summer Games in Beijing in 2008 by over ten billion US dollars. Even a year

after the Games in Sochi, the actual total costs have not been disclosed and it is possible that they will never be published: they likely exceed the final estimates significantly. In this way, the 2014 Games in Sochi represent an extreme example of regional policy: about 115,000 US dollars per capita of Sochi were invested in the region. Every Russian citizen thus implicitly passed up close to 350 US dollars in state funding.

In the face of this bonanza, one would think that the inhabitants of Sochi considered themselves lucky. New roads, additional rail connections, a modern airport, reliable electricity supply, new jobs, extra tourist offers — what more could they wish for? Still, frustration and disappointment could be noticed all around. The authorities promised everything under the sun. Kindergartens and schools, a new motorway access road, a connection to the gas grid.

But the iron law of mega events prevailed: only what directly

12 — Die neue Bahntrasse verbindet die Küste mit
dem Berggebiet in Krasnaja Poljana.

13 — Das Biathlon- und Skilanglaufzentrum «Laura».

14 — Ein Mitarbeiter des Organisationskomitees führt ein Telefongespräch. Im Hintergrund die provisorische Zuschauertribüne der Skisportwettbewerbe in «Rosa Khutor».

15 — Mit Planen und Postern werden Baustellen kaschiert oder Bauruinen versteckt.

16 — Die Winterolympiade, in sommerlicher Atmosphäre, am Strand von Sotschi.

17 — Nur einige hundert Meter vom luxuriösen Olympiapark entfernt sind die Quartierstraßen wieder einfache Schotterpisten.

Allzu sehr haben die Verantwortlichen das Blaue vom Himmel herab versprochen. Kindergärten und Schulen, eine Auffahrt auf die neue Autobahn, ein Anschluss an das Gasnetz.

Aber so ist das eherne Gesetz der Großanlässe: Nur das, was unmittelbar dem Event dient, wird auch gebaut. In Sotschi hat dies zu einer räumlich stark polarisierten Entwicklung geführt: Einige Quartiere sind von Grund auf um- oder neu gebaut worden, so auch das von Julia Erofeeva. In andere hingegen wurde nichts oder kaum etwas investiert: Die Schotterwege, die erratische Stromversorgung, das schlechte Trinkwasser haben sich nicht verbessert, die medizinische Versorgung oder die Schulen auch nicht. Stattdessen liessen die Organisatoren Sichtschutzwände entlang der großen Straßen bauen, damit der unbefleckte olympische Blick nicht durch die Unvollkommenheit der Stadt gestört werde. Und so wie diese Wände den Besucher von der eigentlichen Stadt trennen, so trennen sie auch die Bürgerinnen und Bürger von den Spielen. «Die Spiele sind nicht für uns, die sind für die anderen», meint eine Bewohnerin.

Diese ominösen «anderen» werden nie benannt, aber doch weiß jeder, wer sie sind. Putins Intimus Arkadi Rotenberg beispielsweise wickelte über seine Unternehmen ein Portfolio von 3,4 Milliarden US-Dollar an staatlichen Aufträgen ab. Der Chef der russischen staatlichen

Eisenbahn und Duzfreund Putins, Wladimir Jakunin, bekam den größten Auftrag: den Bau einer Schienenverbindung vom Flughafen in die Berge, zum Wintersportressort Krasnaja Poljana. Die Mechanismen für persönliche Bereicherung sind jeweils ähnlich. Entweder werden unliebsame Akteure durch staatlich sanktionierte Schikanen unter Druck gesetzt, um so eine günstige Aneignung ihres Besitzes zu erzwingen, oder es werden Auftragssummen künstlich aufgebläht, um so jeder Anspruchsgruppe einen entsprechenden Anteil am Kuchen zu garantieren. Wer in Ungunst fällt, muss das Feld räumen. Die Brüder Bilalow mussten ihre Anteile an einem Skigebiet in Krasnaja Poljana verkaufen und nach Deutschland emigrieren, nachdem Achmed Bilalow bei Putin in Ungnade gefallen war. Eigens bestellte staatliche Inspektoren hatten Schlendrian und Misswirtschaft in Bilalows Bauprojekten festgestellt. Offiziell gibt es jedoch keine Korruption bei den Vorbereitungen auf die Winterspiele. Eine groß angelegte staatliche Untersuchung förderte keinen einzigen Fall von illegalen Zahlungen zu Tage.

Vom Traum zum Alptraum

Für den Traum der perfekten Winterspiele in Sotschi zogen die Verantwortlichen alle Register. Die Namen der Architekten und Planer für Sotschi lesen sich wie das globale Who's who der (Winter-)

serves the event will eventually be built. In Sochi, this has led to a strong geographical split in terms of development: some residential areas were renovated or newly built from scratch, like the one where Yulia Erofeeva's house used to stand. Other areas, however, have hardly seen any investments: the gravel roads, erratic electricity and bad drinking water supply have hardly improved, neither has the health-care system nor the schools. Instead, the organisers built screen walls along the major roads so that the immaculate view of the Olympic Games would not be disturbed by the imperfections of the city. These walls separate the visitors from the actual city as much as they separate the inhabitants from the Games. 'The Games are not for us, they are for the others', said a local woman.

The ominous 'others' are never named, but everyone knows who they are. Putin confidant Arkady Rotenberg, for instance, handled a portfolio of 3.4 billion US dol-

lars in government contracts via his company. The head of the Russian Railways and Putin's close friend Vladimir Yakunin won the biggest contract: for the construction of a railway connection linking the airport to the mountains and to the winter sports resort of Krasnaya Polyana. The mechanisms in place for personal enrichment are always similar. Either adversaries are put under pressure by state-sanctioned harassment to force them to give up their property at a low price, or the contract volumes are artificially inflated to guarantee each and every group of stakeholders its share of the pie. Whoever falls into disgrace has to cede the field. The Bilalov brothers had to sell their share in a skiing resort in Krasnaya Polyana and emigrate to Germany after Akhmed Bilalov had fallen into disfavour with Putin. State-appointed inspectors had observed inefficiency and mismanagement in Bilalov's construction projects. Officially, there have not

12 — The new railroad tracks connect the coast with the mountain resort in Krasnaya Polyana.

13 — The Laura biathlon and cross-country skiing centre.

14 — A staff member of the organising committee talking on the phone. In the background, the makeshift grandstands for the skiing competitions in Rosa Khutor.

15 — Tarpaulins and posters cover up construction sites and unfinished buildings.

16 — Winter Olympics in a summery atmosphere, at the beach in Sochi.

17 — Just a few hundred metres from the luxurious Olympic Park, the district's streets are merely gravel roads.

Sportszene: Ecosign aus Whistler bei Vancouver gestaltete die Bewerbung für die Winterspiele mit, Drees & Sommer aus Stuttgart traten als Projektmanager für den olympischen Park auf, das Architekturbüro Populous entwarf das Olympiastadion Fischt, die deutschen Ingenieurbüros Gurgel + Partner und Kohlbecker zeichneten für die Bobbahn beziehungsweise die Sprungschanzen verantwortlich. Internationale Hotelbetreiber wie Radisson, Hyatt, Swissôtel, Marriott oder Accor haben Häuser in Sotschi und Umgebung eröffnet.

Doch der olympische Traum hat sich für die Organisatoren und Investoren wie auch für die Bevölkerung sehr schnell in einen Alptraum verwandelt. Die Straßen- und Schienentrasse zwischen dem Flughafen in Adler an der Küste und den Skiliften in den Bergen für den liebevoll «Schwalbe» (lastotschka) genannten Zug war mit mehr als zehn Milliarden US-Dollar das größte Projekt und kostete allein fast doppelt so viel wie die gesamten Investitionen für die Winterspiele 2010 in Vancouver. Sie war wohl das Projekt mit den folgenschwersten Eingriffen in die Umwelt. Die massiven Pfeiler, die die Trasse tragen, wurden in das Bett des Flusses Mzymta gerammt und ziehen sich entlang des Tals den Berg nach oben. Der Fluss selbst wurde über lange Strecken verbaut und begradigt, große Mengen Kies wurden für die Bauarbeiten direkt aus dem Flussbett entnommen und eine Serie an Tunneln in die Berge

gefräst. Die größte Ironie dabei: Die notdürftige Renaturierung des Flusslaufs, die erst durch internationalen Druck überhaupt zustande kam, wird nun als eine der größten Errungenschaften des Nachhaltigkeitskonzepts der Winterspiele gepriesen.

Die Schwalbe war das Rückgrat des Transportkonzepts für die Winterspiele. Doch die Behändigkeit ihrer Namensgeberin fehlt ihr. Das träge Ungetüm schleicht, fast leer, den Berg hinauf und hinab und braucht für die Strecke von 50 Kilometern gut 40 Minuten. Dabei fährt sie jetzt, nach den Spielen, gerade fünf Mal am Tag. Als Alternative zum Auto, die sie einmal sein sollte, ist sie gescheitert. Inzwischen ist der einst so vollmundig gepriesene Zugvogel zum Pleitegeier geworden.

Zahlreichen Hotels geht es nicht anders. Allein 14 Fünf-Sterne-Hotels gibt es inzwischen in der Region Sotschi – 13 davon wurden für den Großanlass gebaut. Doch nicht alle Unterkünfte wurden rechtzeitig zur Eröffnung fertig, was für großen Spott in der twitternden Journalistengemeinde sorgte. Fotos von falsch montierten Heizkörpern, fehlenden Toilettentrennwänden und Treppen, die ins Nichts führten, machten die Runde. Manche fanden beim ersten Betreten ihres Zimmers bereits einen anderen Gast schlafend im Bett vor; andere mussten erst die Schutzfolien von ihren Fenstern abziehen. Während der Spiele

---

been any known cases of corruption during the preparations for the Winter Games. A large-scale government investigation did not bring a single case of illegal payments to light.

A dream turns into a nightmare

The authorities pulled out all the stops for their dream of perfect Winter Games in Sochi. The names of the architects and heads of planning for the event in Sochi read like a list of the who's who in the (winter) sporting scene. Ecosign from Whistler, near Vancouver, contributed to the bid for the Winter Games, Drees & Sommer from Stuttgart, Germany, were the project managers of the Sochi Olympic Park, architecture firm Populous designed the Fisht Olympic Stadium, the German engineering consultants Gurgel + Partner and Kohlbecker were in charge of the bobsleigh track and the ski jumps. International hotel operators such as Radisson,

Hyatt, Swissôtel, Marriott or Accor have opened hotels in Sochi and surroundings.

But the Olympic dream quickly turned into a nightmare for the organisers, investors and the population. The combined road and rail link between the Sochi International Airport and the ski resorts in the mountains, for a train affectionately called 'swallow' or lastochka, was, with a budget of over ten billion US dollars, the biggest project and cost almost twice as much as the overall investments for the Winter Games in Vancouver in 2010. It was probably also the project with the most severe environmental impact. The massive pillars that carry the tracks were piled into the riverbed of the Mzymta river and move along the valley up into the mountains. The river itself was obstructed and straightened, large volumes of gravel needed for the construction were directly taken from the riverbed and a series of tunnels were carved into the mountains. The biggest irony

of all: the poor renaturation of the river, which was implemented only upon international pressure, is now praised as one of the biggest achievements of the sustainability concept of the Winter Games.

The 'swallow' was meant to be the backbone of the transport concept for the Winter Games. But it lacks the agility of its namesake. This lethargic monstrosity creeps up and down the mountain almost unmanned and takes a good 40 minutes to cover a distance of 50 kilometres. And now, after the Games, there are only five trains a day. The railroad has failed to become an alternative to the car. The swift swallow has become a lame duck.

Numerous hotels are suffering the same fate. The Sochi region has a total of 14 five-star hotels – 13 of which were built for the major sports event. However, not all accommodations were completed in time for the opening of the Games, which led to great mockery by the journalism community on Twitter.

18 — In der Bergregion rund um Krasnaja Poljana
wurde ein Touristenort mit vierspuriger Hauptstraße
aus dem Boden gestampft.

19 — Bahntrasse, Schnellstraße, Bahnhof und
Busterminal: Die Landschaft und das Flussbett der
«Mzymta» sind radikal angepasst worden.

20 — Skisprunganlage «RusSki Gorki» in Esto-Sadok.

21 — Olympiapark mit Überwachung aus der Luft.

waren die Hotels voll ausgelastet. Die mehreren zehntausend Freiwilligen, die während der Wettkämpfe Herz, Gesicht und Seele der Spiele waren, mussten in Quartieren weit weg von den Austragungsorten untergebracht werden.

Die verspielt wirkende Architektur der Bauten – mit Türmchen und Säulen machen manche Märchenschlössern Konkurrenz – täuscht aber über die harte ökonomische Realität hinweg. Die Konkurrenz um Gäste für die zahlreichen Betten ist enorm. Die Hotelkapazität in Sotschi hat sich durch die Winterspiele fast verdoppelt. Insgesamt 42 000 Hotelzimmer in verschiedenen Kategorien musste Sotschi für die Winterspiele zur Verfügung stellen – mehr als doppelt so viele wie der tourismusstärkste Schweizer Kanton Graubünden. Diese sind nun bei Weitem nicht ausgelastet: Selbst das Doppelzimmer im glänzend neuen Fünf-Sterne-Hotel Marriott in Krasnaja Poljana ist in der Hochsaison für 120 US-Dollar pro Nacht inklusive Frühstück zu bekommen. Das günstigste Fünf-Sterne-Haus bietet dasselbe Paket für gerade einmal 45 US-Dollar an. Dazu noch ein Tagesskipass für 35 US-Dollar und der Gesamtpreis sieht eher nach Bansko, Bulgarien, als nach den Vergleichsgrößen St. Moritz oder Zermatt aus.

Die größten Sorgen bereitet jedoch die Nachnutzung der sechs Stadien und der Schneesportanlagen. Die Anlagen sind nach den Spielen an das Sportministerium übergegangen, das mit geschätzten Unterhaltskosten zwischen 75 und 125 Millionen US-Dollar pro Jahr rechnet. Ein zwischenzeitlich angedachter Abbau und Wiederaufbau von Stadien an anderen Orten wurde als nicht machbar verworfen: Er war schlicht zu teuer. Die Rede ist nun von Messehallen, doch ist der Umbau vom Stadion zur Ausstellungshalle ein nicht unbedingt offensichtlicher und vor allem keineswegs kostengünstiger Weg. Offen bleibt ohnehin die Frage, welche Messen dort stattfinden sollen, da das Zielpublikum vor allem in Moskau und St. Petersburg sitzen würde.

Zunächst ist der Blick jedoch auf die Formel 1 gerichtet, die seit 2014 mit einem Grand Prix auf dem Gelände des olympischen Parks gastiert. Eine Nachnutzung der Anlagen findet dadurch jedoch nur ganz begrenzt statt: Die Stadien werden bestenfalls als Kulisse gebraucht. Stattdessen wurde eine eigene Tribüne für die Formel-1-Besucher gebaut. Das Olympiastadion wird für die Fußball-WM 2018 als Spielort umgerüstet: Aber mehr als fünf, sechs Fußballspiele werden dort kaum ausgetragen werden. Dafür werden jedoch erst einmal 100 Millionen US-Dollar an Umbaukosten fällig. Allgemein herrscht, wie so oft, Ratlosigkeit am Morgen nach dem großen Ereignis.

Der Wille zur Umgestaltung Sotschis zeigt eine Gigantomanie, die selbst für russische Massstäbe ungewöhnlich ist. Der Umfang der Investitionen stellt alle bisherigen Großprojekte

Pictures of incorrectly installed heaters, missing partition walls in restrooms and stairs that led nowhere made the rounds. Some people even found another guest sleeping in the hotel bed when they first entered their room, others had to take the protective foil off the windows upon arrival. During the Games, the hotels were booked to capacity. Several tens of thousands of volunteers, who formed the heart, face and soul of the Games, had to be accommodated in quarters far away from the venues.

The seemingly playful architecture of the buildings – turrets and pillars made them look like fairy-tale castles – belies the tough economic reality. The competition to fill the available beds with guests is fierce. The hotel capacity in Sochi has almost doubled due to the Winter Games. Sochi had to provide a total of 42,000 hotel rooms of different categories for the Winter Games – more than twice as much as the Swiss canton of Grisons, a tourism hotspot. The accommodations are far from being used to capacity now. A double room in the new and shiny five-star Marriott hotel in Krasnaya Polyana is available in high season for only 120 US dollars a night, including breakfast. The cheapest five-star hotel offers the same for only 45 US dollars. A one-day ski pass is available for 35 US dollars and the total costs make you think more of Bulgarian ski resort Bansko than comparable Swiss resorts like St. Moritz or Zermatt.

The biggest problem, however, is the continued use of the six stadiums and the snow sports facilities. After the Games, they were handed over to the Ministry of Sports, which estimates that annual maintenance costs will run up to between 75 and 135 million US dollars. The plan to dismantle the stadiums and rebuild them in other locations was soon dismissed because it was simply too expensive. Now there is talk of exhibition halls, even though the conversion of stadiums into exhibition halls is for one thing not necessarily obvious nor is it cost-efficient. Also the question as to what kind of exhibitions would be held there remains unanswered as the target audience primarily resides in Moscow or St. Petersburg.

At the moment, the focus is on the Formula 1. Since 2014, the Olympic Park has hosted the Grand Prix on its premises. This does not mean, however, that the facilities are fully used: the stadiums are at best a piece of scenery. Even an extra grandstand was built for the visitors of the Formula 1 race. The Olympic stadium will be modified to be used as a venue for the 2018 FIFA World Cup, but it is unlikely that more than five or six football games will be held there. The modifications, however, will cost another 100 million US dollars. The general feeling on the morning after the major event is, as so often, one of confusion.

The intention to remodel Sochi is an example of megalomania that

der post-sowjetischen Zeit in den Schatten. Die Konsequenzen waren so fatal wie vorhersehbar. Durch den enormen Zeitdruck beim Bau der notwendigen Infrastruktur, oft noch verschärft durch bürokratische Willkür und Vetternwirtschaft, besteht das Haupterbe der Spiele in überdimensionierter Infrastruktur bei mangelhafter Bauqualität zu überteuerten Preisen.

Trotz der exorbitanten Investitionen sind deshalb viele Bewohner Sotschis unzufrieden: Sie sehen den Nutzen der Extravaganz für ihr Alltagsleben nach den Spielen nicht. Im Gegenteil, wurden doch die verbleibenden Filetstücke an der Schwarzmeerküste und in den Bergen an auswärtige Investoren verscherbelt und bleiben damit in Zukunft den zahlenden Gästen vorbehalten. Für den ausländischen Beobachter mögen die Winterspiele 2014 in Sotschi ein vergängliches Lehrstück über die Auswüchse von Russlands Geltungsdrang und die Konsequenzen neopatrimonialer Staatspolitik sein; für die russische Führung eine Gelegenheit, das Land für zwei Wochen von seiner modernisierten Schokoladenseite zu zeigen; für die Athleten und Verbände der sportliche Höhepunkt für die Momente des Wettkampfs. Aber für Julia Erofeeva und ihre Nachbarn haben sie das Leben auf Jahrzehnte verändert. Ob zum Guten, dafür bleibt die russische Regierung den Beweis schuldig.

is unusual even for Russian standards. The investment volume exceeds that of any other major project in post-Soviet times to date. And the consequences are as fatal as predictable. Due to the enormous time constraints during the construction of the necessary infrastructure, often aggravated by bureaucratic despotism and nepotism, the primary legacy of the Games consists of oversized infrastructure with poor construction quality at inflated prices.

Despite the exorbitant investments, many of Sochi's citizens are unhappy: they do not see any use for this extravaganza in their everyday lives after the Games. On the contrary, the remaining strips of land along the Black Sea coast and in the mountains have been sold off cheaply to foreign investors and will thus be reserved for paying visitors in the future. In the eyes of a foreign observer, the 2014 Winter Games in Sochi might be a transient example for Russia's excessive desire for recognition and a consequence of a neo-patrimonial state; for Russia's leadership they were an opportunity to present the modernised country in its best light for two weeks; for the athletes and sports associations the Olympics were moments of sporting and competition glory. But for Yulia Erofeeva and her neighbours, life has been changed for decades to come. The Russian government has failed to show that it has changed for the better.

18 — In the mountain region around Krasnaya Polyana, a tourist resort complete with a four-lane main road was built from scratch.

19 — Railroad tracks, a motorway, a train station and a bus terminal: the landscape and the Mzymta river bed were altered drastically.

20 — The RusSki Gorki ski-jump venue in Esto-Sadok.

21 — The Olympic Park with aerial surveillance.

22 — View across the Olympic Park to the Bolshoy Ice Dome, one of six newly built stadiums along the coast of Adler, Sochi.

23 — Major marketing efforts ensure that the main sponsors of the Olympics are omnipresent.

24 — Access to the new Olympic Park Railway Station in Adler, Sochi.

25 — Not far from the Olympic Park, tarpaulins cover up the bare structures of unfinished buildings.

22 — Blick durch den Olympiapark in Richtung
«Bolschoi-Eispalast», eines von sechs neu
gebauten Stadien an der Küste von Sotschi-Adler.

23 — Die olympischen Hauptsponsoren sind mit
riesigem Marketingaufwand omnipräsent.

24 — Zugang zum neuen Bahnhof «Olympic Park
Railway Station» in Sotschi-Adler.

25 — Unweit des Olympiaparks werden Neubau-
ruinen mit Planen kaschiert.

Martin Müller (geboren 1982 in Pfarrkirchen, Deutschland) ist Professor für Humangeographie an der Universität Zürich. Er hat seit 2001 insgesamt mehr als zwölf Monate für Forschungsarbeiten in Russland verbracht und spricht fließend Russisch. Ab 2009 dokumentierte er die Vorbereitungen und Nachwehen der Winterspiele in Sotschi. Seine Forschung beschäftigt sich mit der Planung und den Auswirkungen von Großveranstaltungen. Er ist zu diesem Thema auch publizistisch tätig, unter anderem in der NZZ, der ZEIT, im Tages-Anzeiger und in Le Temps. Sein Geheimtipp für einen Besuch in Sotschi: Mit Zelt und Rucksack einige Tage durch den Kaukasus zu laufen ist atemberaubender als jegliche olympische Bauten. Oder ansonsten eben ins Fünf-Sterne-Marriott – für 40 Schweizer Franken die Nacht während der Wandersaison. www.martin-muller.net

Martin Müller (born in Pfarrkirchen, Germany, in 1982) is professor for Human Geography at the University of Zurich. Since 2001 he has spent over twelve months in Russia for research purposes and is fluent in Russian. From 2009 he has documented the preparations for and the aftermath of the Winter Games in Sochi. In his research, he deals with the planning and impact of mega events. He also publishes on this topic, among others for the Swiss daily newspapers *Neue Zürcher Zeitung*, *Tages-Anzeiger* and *Le Temps* and the German weekly *Die Zeit*. His insider tip for a visit to Sochi: going backpacking through the Caucasus and camping out for a few days is more breathtaking than visiting any of the Olympic sites. You can also book a room at the five-star Marriott – for 40 Swiss francs (roughly 40 US dollars) a night during the hiking season. www.martin-muller.net

BRUNO HELBLING, FOTOGRAF

Im Bereich der Design- und Architekturfotografie ist Bruno Helbling (1971) schon länger bekannt. Aufgewachsen in Männedorf am Zürichsee, machte er einige berufliche Umwege, bevor er sich seinen Jugendtraum, Fotograf zu werden, verwirklichte.

Nach vierjähriger Ausbildung an der Berufsschule für Gestaltung in Zürich folgten weitere Lehr- und Assistenzjahre in der Schweiz, Australien und Südafrika.

Ab 1998 arbeitet er in Zürich, mit eigenem Studio und auf selbständiger Basis. Seither fotografiert Bruno Helbling für internationale Kunden im redaktionellen sowie im Werbebereich. Daneben realisiert er auch freie Fotoarbeiten zu unterschiedlichen Themen.

DANK

Athen: Costas Lakafossis, Werner van Gent, Ostin Pando und einige geduldige Sicherheitsleute.

Berlin: Amely Okonnek, Jürgen Langhammer, Rüdiger Herzog, Peter Dittmann, André Thiesing und die Berliner Bäder-Betriebe, Elke Commichau (Regattastrecke Berlin-Grünau), Lutz Imhof (Olympiapark Berlin). Peter Mahlow für seine Geduld und das tolle Interview.

Sarajevo: Ahmed Burić, Faruk Boric für ein fantastisches Interview, Nenad Stojanovic, Muhamed Sabic und alle Bewohner des Olympischen Dorfes.

Turin: Francesco Pastorelli, Simona Cerrato, Marco Destefanis für wertvolle Unterstützung und Kontakte, Laura Elina Larmo, Antonio De Sanctis im Bobdress.

Peking: Cynthia He für die grandiose Koordination, Sammi Zhang, Barbara Lüthi, Chou Tao, Annie Jiang, Majin der Alleskönner, Patrick Schnieper.

Sotschi: Martin Müller, Ivo und Jessica Mijnssen, Semyon Simonov, Svetlana Gannushkina, Tatiana Konakova, Daniel Wechlin und alle gastfreundlichen Russen, die wir in Sotschi getroffen haben.

DANKESCHÖN

Mein besonderer Dank geht an Maximiliane Okonnek für die großartige Unterstützung, meine ganze Familie, Pierre Kellenberger für Engagement und Tatkraft, Michaela Chiaki Ripplinger und Team für fundierte Übersetzung und Lektorat, Stefan und Ewa Rotzler für die Begeisterungsfähigkeit und großartige Unterstützung, David Marold, Markus Joachim, Peter Hofstetter, Lars Egert für die Gestaltung der Publikation, Daniela Funk, Mirko Beetschen und alle, die das Projekt unterstützt haben.

BRUNO HELBLING, PHOTOGRAPHER

Bruno Helbling (born in 1971) has been a name in design and architecture photography for a while. Born and raised in Männedorf on Lake Zurich, he took some professional detours before finally realising his childhood dream of becoming a photographer.

After studying photography at Berufsschule für Gestaltung in Zurich for four years, he worked as an assistant to various photographers in Switzerland, Australia and South Africa.

Since 1998, he has been based in Zurich, working from his own studio as a freelancer. Bruno Helbling shoots for international publications and advertising. He also works on independent photography series on various topics.

ACKNOWLEDGEMENTS

Athens: Costas Lakafossis, Werner van Gent, Ostin Pando and a number of patient security staff.

Berlin: Amely Okonnek, Jürgen Langhammer, Rüdiger Herzog, Peter Dittmann, André Thiesing and Berliner Bäder-Betriebe, Elke Commichau (regatta course Berlin-Grünau), Lutz Imhof (Olympiapark Berlin). Peter Mahlow for being so patient and the terrific interview.

Sarajevo: Ahmed Burić, Faruk Boric for a fantastic interview, Nenad Stojanovic, Muhamed Sabic and all inhabitants of the Olympic Village.

Turin: Francesco Pastorelli, Simona Cerrato, Marco Destefanis for his valuable support and contacts, Laura Elina Larmo, Antonio De Sanctis in a bobsleigh uniform.

Beijing: Cynthia He for the best coordination imaginable, Sammi Zhang, Barbara Lüthi, Chou Tao, Annie Jiang, jack-of-all-trades Majin, Patrick Schnieper.

Sochi: Martin Müller, Ivo and Jessica Mijnssen, Semyon Simonov, Svetlana Gannushkina, Tatiana Konakova, Daniel Wechlin and all of the hospitable Russians we met on our trip to Sochi.

SPECIAL THANKS

Maximiliane Okonnek for her amazing support, my whole family, Pierre Kellenberger for his commitment and energy, Michaela Chiaki Ripplinger and team for their knowledgeable translation and copy-editing work, Stefan and Ewa Rotzler for their passion and great support, David Marold, Markus Joachim, Peter Hofstetter, Lars Egert for the design of the publication, Daniela Funk, Mirko Beetschen and everybody who has supported this project.

IMPRINT

Olympic Realities
Sechs Städte nach dem Großanlass
Six Cities after the Games

www.olympicrealities.info
www.helblingfotografie.ch

Editor: Bruno Helbling

Photography: Bruno Helbling
2012–2014

With contributions by: Werner van
Gent, Peter Dittmann, Ahmed Burić,
Francesco Pastorelli, Barbara
Lüthi, Martin Müller

Translation from German into
English (Athens, Berlin,
Beijing, Sochi): Michaela Chiaki
Ripplinger, Laura Scheifinger,
Daniela Razocher

Translation from Italian into
German (Turin): Simona Cerrato

Translation from Bosnian into
German (Sarajevo): Ivana Stojić

Translation from Bosnian into
English (Sarajevo): Azra Radaslić

Copy editing: Michaela Chiaki
Ripplinger, Laura Scheifinger,
Daniela Razocher

Proofreading: Sabrina Steinmann

Graphic design: Lars Egert

Printing and binding: Holzhausen
Druck GmbH

Library of Congress Cataloging-
in-Publication data

A CIP catalog record for this
book has been applied for at the
Library of Congress.

Bibliographic information
published by the German National
Library

The German National Library
lists this publication in the
Deutsche Nationalbibliografie;
detailed bibliographic data
are available on the Internet
at http://dnb.dnb.de.

This publication is also
available as an e-book.

ISBN PDF 978-3-0356-0643-0
ISBN EPUB 978-3-0356-0651-5

© 2015 Birkhäuser Verlag GmbH,
Basel, P.O. Box 44, 4009 Basel,
Switzerland

Part of Walter de Gruyter GmbH,
Berlin/Boston

Printed on acid-free paper
produced from chlorine-free pulp.
TCF ∞

Printed in Austria
ISBN 978-3-0356-0631-7

9 8 7 6 5 4 3 2 1
www.birkhauser.com